Broadway Christian Church
Real Solutions for Caring for You...
Ketterman, M.D., Grace and Kathy...

P9-DOD-441

0000 7889

REAL SOLUTIONS
for Caring for Your Elderly Parent

REAL SOLUTIONS
for Caring for Your Elderly Parent

Grace Ketterman, M.D.
and
Kathy King, Ph.D.

SERVANT PUBLICATIONS
ANN ARBOR, MICHIGAN

Copyright 2001 by Grace Ketterman and Kathy King
All rights reserved.

Vine Books is an imprint of Servant Publications especially designed to serve
evangelical Christians.

Published by Servant Publications
P.O. Box 8617
Ann Arbor, Michigan 48107

Cover design by Uttley/DouPonce DesignWorks, Sisters, Oregon

01 02 03 04 10 9 8 7 6 5 4 3 2 1

Printed in the United States of America
ISBN 1-56955-251-7

Library of Congress Cataloging-in-Publication Data

Ketterman, Grace H.
  Real solutions for caring for your elderly parent / Grace Ketterman and
Kathy King.
     p. cm.
Includes bibliographical references
   ISBN 1-56955-251-7 (alk. paper)
   1. Aging parents—Care. I. King, Kathy. II. Title.
HQ1063.6 .K48 2001
306.874—dc21

                                                          2001005110

To our parents,
our children,
and our grandchildren

Contents

Acknowledgments

Thank you to friends, family members, and patients who shared their valuable insights. Thanks especially to Patricia Meyers, Diane Balagna, Dr. Steve Jackson, Pat Campbell, and Joyce Bamberger for contributing, helping to read and edit this manuscript, and bringing humor to the process.

Introduction

If you are reading this book, you are likely middle-aged. Remember when forty looked like a near-death experience? When my daughter Kathy, who coauthored this book, turned forty, she got very depressed. But she quit worrying after I asked her to imagine what it feels like to have a *child* turning forty!

Being middle-aged likely means you are in the "middle" of everything—in the middle of helping your older children get through school or start careers and families, in the middle of preparing for retirement (or thinking about it), in the middle of commitments to your career, church, and community.

And then you wake up one day, take a good look at your parents, and discover they are not the same folks who brought you up. They've started to forget things and tell you stories over and over. They seem shorter. Perhaps they're ill, or impatient, or exhibit atypical qualities. They may be having financial difficulties. Their home may be in disrepair. You realize the time has come when your parents might need you to care for them. You are part of what has been called the "sandwich generation," caught between the needs of your children and your aging parents.

I am a child psychiatrist and pediatrician and have been in practice for nearly fifty years. I am the mother of three and the grandmother of four. I have had extensive experience with families and have participated in and with five generations of my own family. My daughter Kathy is a psychologist who has worked with families for twelve years. She is the mother of a twenty-three-year-old son. I joined Kathy's private practice seven years ago after retiring as medical director of a children's psychiatric hospital.

When my publisher asked me to write a book on caring for elderly parents, I asked Kathy to help; I felt a mother-daughter approach would broaden and deepen the perspective on this topic. For the sake of readability, we chose to write in my voice, but we worked as a team in the writing of this book and our contributions were equal. We chose topics based on our shared professional experiences as well as our personal experiences across many generations of our own family.

On May 15, 2000, *Larry King Live* did a segment on the problems of aging and announced that by the year 2030, there will be seventy-five million people in this country over the age of sixty-five; by the year 2050, there will be one million people over one hundred years of age. Most of us will not escape the challenges of aging. We hope the information we've brought together in *Real Solutions for Caring for Your Elderly Parents* will help you prepare for the time when you must become your parents' caregiver.

We wrote this book to help you identify and prevent potential problems, to provide you with practical solutions for those problems, and to encourage you to take exceptional care of yourself, your marriage, and your children to avoid what has come to be labeled "caregiver burden."

As a person in middle age, you have already made safe passage through at least one leg of your life journey. We hope this book will make the rest of your journey smoother.

Chapter One

WHERE ARE YOU GOING AND
WHEN WILL YOU BE BACK?
Encouraging Independence While Setting Limits

Becky's elderly parents still live in their own home. Becky and her husband, Steve, check in with them by phone twice a week just to see what their plans are, how they are feeling, and whether Steve or Becky can be of particular help that week. They keep track of her parents' general schedules and activities. They have chosen, wisely, to be involved in their parents' daily lives *before* the older couple becomes disabled or incompetent. This way they can better discern if and when they need to limit their parents' autonomy.

All of us need to feel a degree of independence in our lives. Perhaps you remember resenting your parents when you were a teenager because they put limits on your independence, constantly questioning your decisions, activities, and friends.

A desire for independence doesn't evaporate when people can no longer take care of themselves because of age-related problems. Imagine how difficult it must be for men and women who have lived independently for fifty years to lose their ability to take care of themselves!

Independence enhances the quality of our lives and likely even affects our longevity. You don't want to limit your parents' independence unnecessarily, but how can you know when leaving them to their own decisions becomes dangerous or self-defeating? How can you monitor and be involved in the details of their lives without being intrusive, patronizing, or controlling?

Older people want—and need—to maintain some level of control over their lives. If you can, find ways to enable your parents to have some say in:

- Making their own financial decisions
- Getting around
- Participating in social events—and choosing which ones they will engage in
- Staying in their own homes
- Attending to their own physical health

Let's explore each of these areas for some practical ways you can help your parents stay independent while at the same time offering them the assistance and protection they may need.

Making Their Own Financial Decisions

Helping your parents will be easier if you can get them to share details about their financial, physical, emotional, spiritual, and social needs. Ask them about their past experiences as their own parents got older. "Your dad died at seventy-five," you might say. "How did he leave things for you? Can we help you get your finances in better order?"

My father and his brothers, because their parents didn't have a will when they died, were angry with each other for years over the disposition of the family farm. My dad couldn't stand the thought of losing the farm, so he borrowed money in the heart of the Depression to buy out his brothers. A will would have made everyone's life easier by sorting out the situation before it became a problem.

Knowing my father's story was one motivation for me and my husband to write a will. We have also talked with our children about how we'd like them to handle our finances when the time comes that we can't handle them ourselves.

Here are some ways you can help your parents maintain a level of independence when it comes to their finances:

1. Encourage them to pay their own bills for as long as possible, even if you are the one making deposits and balancing the checkbook. When it comes time to pay a particular bill, remind your parents to make out the check and note it in their check register. You might also set up a system to help remind them when bills are due, perhaps through a clearly organized monthly file. I've set up an accordion file to keep bills and papers in order for my older sister, Edith. Now she has a specific place to put paperwork, and she makes it a point to check every day for bills that need to be paid on that date.

2. Sit down with your parents before they become disabled and talk with them about their finances. If you don't already know, find out how your parents spend their money. Help them formulate or maintain a budget. Assure them that you want them to live independently for as long as possible. Let them know their well-being is more important than leaving their children money.

3. If your parents need it and can afford it, set up a budget that allows for household help. If their expenses are too high, talk with them about downsizing. Kathy has a friend whose mother, after all the children moved out, sold her house and moved to a very nice one-bedroom townhouse. It was the perfect size for Susan's mom, and much easier for her to handle alone.

4. Find out the location of their safety deposit boxes, financial records, and will; their bank accounts and account numbers; and the names and numbers of any financial advisors, attorneys, or accountants. Be sure to tell them that you want to take care of their legacy, and that to do that in the long run, you need information in the short run.

5. To avoid confusion or squabbling after their death, suggest that they designate jewelry and other valuable or sentimental items to specific children or grandchildren. Also talk with them about what happens to any family heirlooms if a surviving parent remarries.

Joe's wife of thirty-two years died unexpectedly of a heart attack. His two adult sons, Ron and Carl, were devastated, but they were even more devastated when Joe remarried within six months. Joe's first wife had left many beautiful antiques which had been in her family for generations, but she had not specified that they were to go to Ron and Carl.

After Joe died, his second wife ended up with most of these valuable antiques in her possession, and Joe's sons did not acquire them until after her death. Ron and Carl both felt cheated by this long process, and it negatively affected their relationship with their father and stepmother. They resented their father's new wife and felt their father had not stood up for their rights.

6. If your parents are hesitant to discuss or share these details with you, strongly encourage them to discuss them with an attorney or a financial advisor. Setting up a will, or even better, a trust, saves unnecessary taxation and emotional wear and tear on heirs, and ensures that your parents' assets will go where your parents want them to.

Here is how you might approach this conversation:

Patricia: "Mom and Dad, we'd love for you to live forever, but that isn't going to happen. You're almost eighty, and if something happened to you suddenly, none of us know where your papers are or how you've left things."

Dad: "We don't want you kids to have to worry about that. It's all taken care of."

Patricia: "But without knowing anything, we will worry, Dad. When you're gone, we won't be able to ask you anything. Let's talk about things now, while you're here."

You might interview several attorneys or financial planners in order to ensure that your parents speak with someone who is reliable and qualified to address their specific needs. Then give your folks the names and phone numbers. Tell them, "It would be a relief for me to have you talk to Mr. Smith," rather than, "You have to see Mr. Smith." If all else fails, talk to your own attorney about your parents' finances and how you can best be involved to protect them and their assets. Your attorney may be able, for example, to contact your parents' attorney for help in completing financial management.

Getting Around

Driving can be increasingly hazardous for elders as they begin to lose vision and hearing and their reaction time slows down. If you are concerned about your parents' safety while driving, try these ideas:

1. *Ride with them to determine whether their driving is a threat to themselves, other drivers, and pedestrians.* (Nervous? Don't forget that your parents suffered through teaching *you* how to drive!) If you feel your parents are no longer safe drivers, consult either their physician or ophthalmologist. If these doctors agree with you, you may have to firmly insist that a parent stop driving. Some doctors may be willing to be included in this discussion. The blow to your parents' independence, should this be the case, will be eased if you have some alternate plans for their transportation.

2. *Call a local Division of Motor Vehicles near your parents and find out if they offer classes for senior citizens.* Some states have programs to teach seniors how to compensate for some of their physical limitations. If such classes are available, tell your parents about them and encourage them to attend.

3. *Accompany your elderly parents when they go to renew a driver's license.* To ensure that your folks are passing all requirements for license renewal, talk with the examiner about your concerns. If the DMV determines that the license cannot be renewed, you will be there to help your parents cope with this loss.

4. *If and when your parents lose their licenses or are no longer able to drive, volunteer to take them places they need to go.* Be aware that the loss of a driver's license will create a huge burden on both your parents and the rest of your family. In many cities public transportation is poor or nonexistent, severely limiting peoples' freedom and ability to come and go as they please.

Here are some ways you can help your parents make the difficult transition from driver to nondriver:

- Hire a friend or neighbor to drive them to the store or the doctor when needed.
- Arrange for bus or public transportation passes and show your parents how to use them.
- Check in the Yellow Pages for Older Adult Transportation Services (OATS) and see if they have services available in your parents' neighborhood. If they do, they'll have schedules and timetables available.

- Encourage your parents to ask for help. If a neighbor is going to the store anyway, she might, if asked, be happy to pick up a few things for them.
- Be willing to take your parents to social or volunteer activities. To keep resentment at bay, remember all the places they once drove you!
- Ask church members to pick them up for church.
- Encourage parents to give their car to someone special (such as a grandchild) rather than sell it.
- Convert the empty garage to a workshop or hobby room.

Participating in Social Events

Older people often give up on social and physical activities simply because it's much easier to stay home. They may lack the energy to go out, they may be afraid to go out, or they may not be aware of available activities. Depression can also inhibit the desire to stay active.

Help your parents stay involved in life by doing one or more of the following:

1. Provide them with information on volunteer needs, activities in senior citizens' centers, and cultural events—and be willing to accompany them if necessary. Hospitals, elementary schools, and preschools often need volunteers. After her children left home, one of Kathy's friends got involved with an organization that rescues and places abandoned pets.

You may have to tell a parent, "I'll go with you until you are comfortable." Diane initially accompanied her mother to a preschool that utilized older folks as teachers' aides. Her mother, a retired school teacher, got so involved in this program that she developed her own reading preparation curriculum. This program helped her feel that she still had something to offer in her life.

2. *Include your parents in your children's activities and special events.* My grandsons all love it when Grandma and Grandpa come to their baseball games, school plays, or church performances. We encourage our kids to give us plenty of advance notice so we can make the necessary arrangements.

3. *If you don't live near your parents, send them scrapbooks of your kids.* Scrapbooks are becoming very popular, and they are a great way to keep grandparents connected with grandkids. Involve your children. Include:

- Pictures they've drawn
- School papers
- Letters
- Copies of grade cards
- Pictures of friends, teachers, etc.

4. *Encourage your parents to put together a scrapbook for your family.* It might include:

- Stories about their childhood (I remember my grandmother telling me about the excitement of her family's first telephone!)
- Pictures of relatives with names and stories

- Descriptions of family heirlooms and stories about them
- Life lessons grandparents have learned
- Stories about grandchildren as babies

5. Communicate with your parents regularly. Phone calls are incredibly important between grandparents and grandchildren. Give your young children ideas about things they can share with their grandparents. Remind your parents about what's going on in the lives of their grandchildren. For instance: "Mom, your grandson got an A on his math test today. And he made the soccer team! Do you want to congratulate him?"

If both you and your parents have computers, communicate by e-mail. Many retired and elderly people are finding ways to stay connected to family and friends through the Internet and e-mail.

6. Encourage your parents to see friends and to get out regularly for some kind of exercise. Do they like dogs? Dogs provide great incentive for walking!

7. Encourage churches to become more involved with their older parishioners. Jeannette, eighty-five years old, has arranged for a family from her church to pick her up each Sunday. She enjoys being involved in this family's life during these trips and is able to stay active in her church through the help of this kindhearted family.

If your parents are having trouble with transportation to church and insist they don't know anyone to ask, call the church office and ask if someone there would be responsible for getting them to and from services. If not, you may be able to organize a transportation system for the elderly.

Jesus said, "Verily I say unto you, Inasmuch as ye have done it unto one of the least of these my brethren, ye have done it unto me" (Matthew 25:40). Many churches seem to consider their elderly members "the least of these." Those in the sandwich generation need to become activists for the elderly in their churches, providing transportation, setting up visitation schedules or phone calls, arranging for them to receive communion at home, perhaps setting up an adopt-a-grandparent program.

Staying in Their Own Homes

Encourage your parents to live in their own home as long as financially and physically possible. I am extremely comfortable after years in my home because I know where the light switches are and where to find the cereal. Your parents probably feel the same way about their home.

Consider the following ideas to help your parents remain in their home as long as possible:

1. Offer to help with household tasks. Help beautify the house and take care of repairs. One of my sisters always appreciated her daughter coming over in the spring to help her plant flowers. Encourage your kids to help, too. Grandchildren are gifts from God and we should encourage them to participate in these efforts. I have great memories of my grandson Andy, Kathy's son, coming over to help me decorate for Christmas every year.

If one sibling lives closer to Mom and Dad, the other siblings can find ways to support and assist him or her in caring for parents in practical ways. If one of your siblings is your parents' primary caregiver, offer that person lots of emotional support and do your best to visit your parents as often as possible. Provide financial assistance for weekend respite care or spend occasional weekends yourself.

One of Kathy's dear friends, Joyce, lives in Alaska, while her elderly parents and her brother live in Kansas City. Her brother is a physician and she is an attorney. Joyce feels guilty that her brother, because of his physical proximity, has to do more for their parents than she is able to do.

She believes that her mom's life, in particular, would be better if they lived closer. Joyce would make sure the house was better arranged for her mom to get around in, and she'd go out of her way to get her mom more socially involved. Living in Anchorage makes that impossible.

Joyce does as much as she can by long distance, however. She probably talks more to her parents than her brother does—she tries to call twice a week. She is also currently helping them decide on a retirement location. Getting the most current information available through the Internet, she relays her findings to her folks.

She has also reviewed all her dad's trusts, investments, and paperwork. She helped him find an estate attorney in Kansas City and stays in contact with that attorney. Joyce believes that the best thing distant adult children can do for their parents is to determine their own strengths and use them in whatever way possible. Physical distance may make helping out more difficult, but certainly not impossible.

2. *Ensure that your parents are eating properly by helping them make up menus and grocery lists.* Your local grocery store offers many prepackaged, easy-to-prepare meals, most of which provide at least minimally adequate nutrition, especially when taken with daily vitamin supplements. Check packaging to determine nutritional value. Several books listed in Appendix A offer good information regarding nutrition. In addition, many communities offer services such as Meals on Wheels to older adults.

3. *Encourage simplification.* Microwave ovens are a godsend, and we should teach our parents to use them!

Simplifying doesn't always come easily. Doris and Roy are an elderly couple who always prided themselves on formal dinner times with a fully set table. Their son Don did convince them they deserved to take life easier by making dinner a little more informal, but it took some time. While it may be initially difficult for your parents to change long-established habits such as using china and silverware at meals, you might remind them that disposable plates and dinnerware keep dishwashing to a minimum.

Many elderly people become pack rats. Often the "stuff" they collect is harmless, but it can become dangerous. Too much paper can become a fire hazard. Too much furniture creates a potential for falls. If your parents' safety is at risk, encourage them to get rid of some of their "stuff." If they don't, you may have to do it for them.

How might you approach such a task—and the conversation leading up to it? Here's an example:

Let's suppose Kathy comes to our home for a visit and stumbles over the latest of her dad's acquisitions, a huge curio cabinet. He needs lots of curio cabinets because, of course, he has lots of curios! She realizes that if she can trip over it, her father or I can, too—with far more serious consequences. "You guys have so much furniture in this house," she might say to her dad. "It's looking so cluttered! I remember how nice and orderly it looked when I was growing up, and I miss that. Besides, I tripped over that display cabinet. What if you did the same thing?"

"I know how to get around," her dad says. "And you'll be able to sell all this stuff at the estate sale."

"Well then," Kathy compromises, "how about if we get rid of this old chair over here and move the cabinet out of the way?"

Even though Herb doesn't want to get rid of his things just yet, he's willing to let Kathy move things around to make our home safer and more livable.

Try the same approach with your parents. But don't let them

throw out everything! If the time comes for them to move to a care facility, taking along a few of their favorite pieces to furnish their new space will help make the move easier.

Attending to Their Own Physical Health

Your parents have been taking care of their own health needs for a long time. Are they still capable of doing so? You can keep an eye on their health in the following ways:

1. Meet their physicians and insist they call you about any concerns or changes in your parents' health. If your parents aren't willing to let you accompany them to doctor appointments, contact their doctors on a regular basis on your own. You can stay in touch with your parents' physicians even if you don't live in the area.

My father-in-law was diabetic, had poor vision and poor hearing, and refused to go to the doctor. All his children insisted that he make an appointment, but he refused. One day I finally said, "OK, next Tuesday I'll come get you and we're going to the doctor." The decision was out of his hands, and he actually seemed relieved and happy to comply. You may find the same to be true for a parent reluctant to visit the doctor.

2. Help parents organize medications, and check that medications are taken correctly. Organize their pillboxes and set timers to remind them of scheduled doses. If your parents are no longer able to be responsible for their own medications, explore visiting nurse or licensed practical nurse resources in their area. Eventually, one or both of your parents may require assisted living. But until then, with proper instruction, even a lay person can ensure they receive their medications correctly.

3. Be aware of your parents' personal hygiene. Is the laundry getting done? Are your parents bathing or showering regularly? Move washers and dryers to the main floor, if possible, to make it easier for them to keep up with the laundry. Help install a new shower, or affix safety bars in a bathtub to encourage them to practice better personal hygiene.

Independence is among the most valued of our possessions. Encourage your parents to maintain theirs as long as is reasonably possible, even if it means personal inconvenience for you. The sense of safety that comes from living in a familiar environment will increase the quality of their lives.

Chapter Two

WHEN EVEN DOWN LOOKS UP
Attending to Grief and Depression

My husband, Herb, recently experienced a flare-up of a cancer he'd been battling successfully for over ten years. He became very ill, and we came face-to-face with our mortality in a way we never had before. I struggled to know how to offer him hope and keep him from despair, but I was dealing with my own feelings of helplessness and frustration. I felt frightened, and very sad for myself and our children and grandchildren. How could I comfort my husband when I was feeling so sad myself?

During the time I was grieving over the possible loss of my husband, I gained great comfort from my children and grandchildren. My youngest grandchildren made frequent visits. Kathy and I sat down and developed a plan for my care if Herb should die. My children understood and accepted my sadness, but did not try to "fix" it.

Thankfully, Herb's cancer is once again in remission, but the experience threw our family into grief. If just a warning of the death of a loved one causes us to mourn so deeply, how much more intense will our grief be when we finally lose that person?

As people age, grief becomes a part of life. Sometimes the grief can lead to depression, and if left untreated, depression can result in loss of hope and a sense of purpose in life.

East of the Mountains, a best-selling novel by David Guterson, explores the depression that many older people experience after the death of a spouse or when they learn that they themselves have a terminal illness. In this well-written novel, a recently widowed doctor has just learned he has terminal cancer. As a physician, he knows exactly what kind of death he can expect and what kind of burden he will be to his daughter in his illness. Rather than face all that, he decides to commit suicide, concocting a scheme that will make it look as if he died an accidental death.

Even though the story is fiction, the circumstances and feelings in the story are very true to life. According to a recent study, older people make up about 12 percent of the population in the United States, but account for 20 percent of all suicides.[1] Understanding the components of grief and depression can help you support and encourage your parents as they navigate these difficult waters.

Understanding Grief

Unlike a depressed person, a person in grief can always identify a definite reason for his or her sorrow—and that reason
always involves loss. Repeated unhealed grief experiences can
eventually develop into chronic depression. Some losses may
be obvious while others are subtle. For example, a mother
whose child becomes estranged from her, in addition to grieving the loss itself, might grieve the loss of how the relationship
should have been or could have been.

An elderly person may grieve the following losses:

- Loss of an era of time (childhood, adolescence, middle age)
- Loss of freedom (due to illness or incapacity)
- Loss of health, virility, and/or faculties
- Loss of ideals or dreams
- Loss of financial security
- Loss of intimacy (belonging to a social group, sexual inti-
  macy)
- Loss of significant loved ones (even pets) through death,
  divorce, or separation (one parent, for example, needing
  nursing home care)
- Loss of faith through anger or bitterness at God, misper-
  ceptions or false expectations of God, or mental deterio-
  ration
- Loss of a feeling of significance or importance

The loss of a lifetime partner is one of the greatest shocks a person can endure. It may encompass many of the losses described above, experienced as a single, overwhelming crush of grief. Many couples who spend their lives together become almost one person. Kathy loves to watch older people dance together because they seem to know each other's every move and fit together perfectly. Losing a partner can be like losing part of ourselves.

Marcos felt that way when he lost his wife, Maria. He hadn't realized how deeply his loss would affect him, and when grief hit, he didn't believe he would ever be able to cope without her. He felt lost even in his own house. He couldn't go into a room without remembering something about Maria and breaking into tears. There were times that he felt absolutely frozen in his grief and unable to help himself. He also remembered and regretted every instance in which he had been impatient or harsh with Maria. At times he wished that God had taken his life, rather than Maria's.

Each of us grieves differently, and we may need different things during times of loss. Marcos' son, Tony, had the insight to ask his dad if he would rather spend some time at Tony's house, be alone, or have Tony stay in the family home for a few days. Marcos insisted he wanted to be alone, but Tony sensed his dad was covering up his loneliness and trying to be strong. He arranged to spend a week at his dad's house. He encouraged Marcos to talk about his feelings and to remember special things about Maria.

After several tries, Tony managed to get his dad to church. They made other quick trips outside the house to the grocery store or the post office. Tony shared his fondest family memories and reminded his dad how happy his mother had been because she and Marcos had been so close. Even after Tony returned to his own family, he stayed in close contact with his dad. He also arranged for several family friends and members of his dad's church to stop by for visits on a regular basis.

Tony encouraged his dad to keep talking about Maria, an exercise that helped Marcos process his feelings. So often others expect grief to end after six weeks or two months or some other magical period of time. This is not how grief works. Marcos recycled through his grief for many months to come, and Tony learned that grief comes in cycles and spirals.

Elizabeth Kubler-Ross originally defined the stages of grief. They include:

- Denial
- Anger/blame
- Guilt and self-pity
- Depression, sadness, helplessness
- Resignation
- Healing[2]

While the person experiencing grief will generally go

through these stages in order, he or she may go through one stage several times. As time goes on, the cycles usually grow farther apart and the spirals less deep.

Grief has no common timetable. Cameron was extremely close to his dad, who died unexpectedly six years ago from a heart attack. After all this time, Cam still misses him and grieves his loss. Imagine the devastation that comes with the loss of a lifetime spouse!

Reactions That Cripple the Grief Process
Urging someone to "get through" grief only delays the process. In order to make life easier for themselves, children often want their parents to remember the good times, accept the reality of the loss, and get out of the denial and anger stages as soon as possible. It's important that you hang in there with your surviving parent—and remember that whatever your mom or dad feels is a normal and healthy response to such a devastating loss.

It will help your parent to hear you acknowledge this. Accepting a grieving person's feelings instead of trying to take the feelings away offers great comfort. Don't tell a grieving parent, "You shouldn't feel that way"; it makes him or her feel wrong for having normal feelings. Grief is not wrong.

Guilt can complicate grief. After his wife's death, Marcos struggled with guilt for mistakes he had made in his marriage.

It was too late to apologize to his wife, so he felt helpless to let go of the guilt. Tony's reminders of how happy Maria had been in the marriage comforted Marcos. His priest also suggested that Marcos try apologizing to Maria in his heart.

Self-pity complicates and prolongs grief, too. Betsy had always gotten attention by feeling sorry for herself. Even as a child, she got sympathy from her family by exaggerating physical hurts. She could make mountains out of molehills and convince others they really were mountains! She saw herself as a victim. No one ever felt as bad about anything and everything as Betsy did.

When her mother died, Betsy took it as a personal attack from God. And no one had ever felt as miserable as Betsy did. She called everyone she knew every day for weeks to talk about her grief. Three years later, she is still wallowing in self-pity. It's no longer really grief.

Both guilt and self-pity become detours in the grief process. They can keep people stuck in grief forever. At times when we or our surviving parent may not see these problems clearly, counseling can help identify them.

If grief never moves through the final stage of healing, it can turn into chronic depression—a truly miserable way to live.

Understanding Chronic Depression

People sometimes overlook depression in older adults because many of its symptoms resemble those of physical problems, such as thyroid disorder, diseases of the blood, or the onset of Alzheimer's disease. Depression can actually be precipitated by physical problems, such as chronic pain or disability.

Occasionally a single life stressor (such as the death of a spouse) can lead to depression. So can feelings of loneliness, poor health, or worry about finances. The stressors that produce depression sometimes cause an imbalance in the chemicals necessary for brain cells to function properly.

An improper combination of medications can also cause depression. If your parents are seeing different doctors for different ailments, one may not know what the other is prescribing. Alcohol, with or without drug interactions, can aggravate depression.

People who have lifelong patterns of helplessness, anger, self-pity, excessive worry, or unwarranted guilty feelings are also susceptible to chronic depression. Negative thinking can keep us depressed and hopeless. Dr. David Burns, in his book *Feeling Good: The New Mood Therapy*, writes that if we think positively and make rational decisions, good feelings will result.[3] In other words, we feel what we think. Negative thinking is a difficult habit to break, but learned ways of thinking can be unlearned.

Depression can become pervasive and circular—Mom is depressed so she doesn't eat well or get enough exercise, which makes her more depressed and less likely to eat and exercise.

Below is a list of the symptoms of depression. The expression of only one or two of these may not be of serious concern, but overall changes in personality or a combination of several of these symptoms may signal depression.

- Loss of interest in formerly pleasurable activities
- Dissatisfaction with life
- Withdrawal from normal activities
- Loss of energy
- Feeling useless or hopeless
- Irritability
- Great concern with health problems
- Sadness and crying spells
- Worry or self-criticism
- Difficulty concentrating or making decisions
- Loss of appetite and weight loss, or overeating with weight gain
- Sleep disturbances or changes in regular sleep patterns, such as sleeping too much or too little
- Failure to maintain good personal grooming and hygiene

Ways to Help Your Depressed Parent

What can you do if your parents are depressed? If you notice symptoms of depression, you can help most by giving them an opportunity to talk about their feelings. "You seem unusually quiet," you might say to get a depressed person started. "Are you feeling sad?" Then try the following:

1. Encourage them to talk by asking questions, acknowledging their feelings ("If I were you, I would be sad, too"), and sharing memories. Kathy once had an eighty-year-old client whose reason for attending counseling sessions was only to reminisce and share the events in her life; she had no one else with whom to do so. The elderly need to vent just as much as the rest of us.

Many parents don't want to feel they are "burdening" their kids. If your parents hesitate to talk with you, find someone they are willing to speak with: one of their friends, a clergyman, a doctor or professional counselor, even if only a time or two. Encourage them to write in a diary or journal as a way to get pent-up feelings out. Or simply give them permission to cry and be sad, assuring them that tears are not a burden to you.

2. Reassure your parents of your unconditional love with hugs, calls, and words. Do this even if they don't reciprocate. Often older adults are uncomfortable with emotions. A friend of mine once told me that he visited his mother weekly for over twenty years. He always ended the visit with a hug and the words, "I love you, Mom." She didn't respond that she loved him until shortly before she died. My friend waited a long time, but finally hearing those words was extremely comforting for him. Don't give up.

3. Encourage your parents to talk with their doctor about their depression. Many good antidepressant medicines are available today. Be aware that antidepressants often take up to three weeks to be effective. If one doesn't work, another might. If a parent's depression persists, consult with medical or psychological resources even if your parent won't. I once had a patient who came in because her depressed elderly mother wouldn't. Between the two of us, we talked her mother into taking medication. She eventually felt good enough to come in for some counseling herself.

4. Ask your parents' advice and value their opinions (even if you don't agree). Proverbs 13:1 says, "A wise son hears his father's instruction" (RSV). You can help counter your parents' depression (particularly their sense that they are no longer important) by consulting with them and including them in your life.

We value our children for who they are. We should value our parents for their wisdom, knowledge, and experience. Do small things you know they like or that help them feel significant—like introducing them to your friends. Kathy is always proud to introduce me as her mother, and I always feel included and valued by her when she does. Such actions not only help our parents, they honor the God who said, "Hearken unto thy father that begat thee, and despise not thy mother when she is old" (Proverbs 23:22).

5. If the depression is related to specific problems, help your parents find solutions for those problems. Edith, my older sister, was very worried about her financial resources and felt helpless to do anything about her concerns. I sat down with her, listed her resources and expenses, assured her that I would help her keep track of her money, and went with her to the bank to set up some different accounts. This simple bit of assistance gave Edith amazing peace of mind.

Life is filled with emotion. Grief and depression are normal responses to loss, and all of us feel these emotions at one time or another. Kathy still remembers coming home from school after her freshman year at college only to have a longtime boyfriend break up with her. What she remembers even more clearly, though, was her dad's response to her grieving: Herb literally sat her down in his lap and rocked her like she was a little girl. So strong and comforting!

You likely have similar memories. As our parents age, each of us has an opportunity to repay them for all the love and comfort they gave us when we were the ones in a place of need.

Chapter Three

WHAT'S MINE NOW MAY <u>NOT</u> BE YOURS LATER!
Addressing Financial Issues

Many families are torn apart after the death of a parent because financial issues were not resolved beforehand. When parents don't plan in advance, even simple estates can take years to be settled. Kathy knows of one family that had to deal with attorneys and probate courts for over ten years. Yet these problems are so easily prevented!

We touched briefly on this issue in chapter one, but decisions about finances are so key to both our own and our parents' peace of mind, we wanted to devote an entire chapter to the discussion.

Helping parents manage their financial resources begins with communication. Again, assure your parents that you are not trying to take over their finances; instead, you want to help them provide for their own financial well-being and protect their legacy.

Helping Parents With Estate Planning

Your parents may be reluctant to participate in a discussion about their finances. Reluctance can be caused by many things, including a denial of mortality, procrastination, an unwillingness to part with what they may perceive as confidential information, and fear of losing control of their assets. Analyzing their financial affairs may even depress your parents as they take an honest look at the end of their lives and realize they don't have what they'd hoped to have.

Sometimes one parent may be more willing than the other to participate in a financial discussion. You need to support the willing parent to express his or her thoughts, and, with legal help, to pursue a financial plan with him or her. The more reluctant parent may then, in time, become involved in these discussions.

Media articles about financial planning can provide a good opening for a discussion about financial issues. No matter how small their estate, your parents need an estate plan—a will or a trust.

You might also ask your parents if they would like your help investing or saving money so they can add to their existing investments. Keep in mind, however, that older people tend to prefer safe investments over large returns—and they like to be kept informed about what their money is doing.

If your parents have a will or trust already, be sure you know where the papers, as well as any tax information, deeds, or insurance policies, are located. If they haven't drawn up a will or trust, tell them you are willing to go with them to a banker, attorney, or financial planner for the purpose of estate planning.

If your parents resist, remind them that wills and trusts prevent unnecessary taxation and can help preserve what money they do have. Kathy and her siblings had to nag, cajole, remind, irritate, and generally become total pests to get their dad to finally work on his trust. The whole family is grateful that he finally accomplished this task. I, in this instance, was the more willing parent and also urged Herb to complete the trust for both of us.

Your parents should know that they can give each of their children up to $10,000 annually as a tax-free gift. This provision in the federal tax code can save families a great deal of money in inheritance taxes if they can take advantage of it. In order to avoid appearing greedy, you might ask a financial advisor to share this information with your parents.

A **will** is the most simple estate planning document. This document designates how property is to be transferred at death to the named beneficiaries. If a person has no will or other estate planning mechanism, his or her property transfers by law to a spouse, children, siblings, or other relatives.

The court process by which property is transferred is called *probate*. Usually, the court appoints a representative for the deceased to make sure the property is transferred as stated in the will, or by the laws of intestate succession if there is no will.

To avoid the expense and delays involved in the probate of a will, your parents may want to transfer property at death by way of a **trust.** Property does not have to go through probate under a trust.

Trusts provide a way for beneficiaries to pay less income and estate taxes. They are also a good way to appoint guardians for minors or other incapacitated persons and financial advisors to manage the assets of the estate. For further information, you may want to talk to your own attorney or to an attorney who specializes in trust agreements. (If you are unfamiliar with any of these terms, find a professional who can explain them to you and then use that contact as a springboard to help your parents begin this process.)

Additional ways to plan for transfer of property include **life insurance policies,** which name a beneficiary at time of death, and **property held in joint tenancy** (such as a joint bank account), which immediately passes to the surviving tenant without going through probate.

To help select an appropriate executor and ensure even distribution of assets, an estate planner needs to have some understanding of family history and family dynamics. If a parent wants to disinherit one of the children, for example, or has remarried after the death or divorce of a spouse, make sure the estate planner has this information.

If your parents are no longer married to each other and one or both have remarried, encourage them to obtain separate legal counsel before signing a will that will affect their livelihood should their current spouse die. I recently heard a sad story about a woman whose husband died when she was in her sixties. A few years later, she remarried a man with one son from his first marriage. She had four children. Her second husband owned his own business and also had some rental property. They were married over twenty years, and many times the wife helped her husband financially in order to keep his business out of bankruptcy.

Eight months prior to his death, the husband had his lawyer draw up a postnuptial agreement that stated she would receive $10,000 upon his death and could live for free in one of his rental properties until her death. The rest of his estate—well over half a million dollars—went to his son.

This poor woman agreed to sign the agreement without talking with any of her children or independent legal counsel. By the time her husband died, her own health had deteriorated so much that she couldn't live alone. Her children had to move her to live near one of them and were forced to apply for disability assistance in order to see that she received the care she needed. This story is a prime example of why adult children must do their best to be involved in their parents' financial decisions.

Protection From Con Artists

Both Kathy and I have heard many sad stories about the elderly and con artists. For years, one of my patients contributed
financially to every single request for donations she got in the
mail. She was seriously draining her financial resources until I
was able to help her narrow the scope of her donations to two
charities that were significant to her.

Fortunately this woman followed my recommendations,
but that is not always the case. Almost daily con artists find
ways to cheat elderly people out of money. Such scams range
from investment schemes to deceitful home repair ploys. Even
religious organizations use deceptive practices.

Kathy knows of one elderly couple who insisted on renting
out some duplexes on their property. Time after time they
rented the apartments to unreliable people. Sadly, all of these
people had one thing in common—they treated this couple as
if they were friends and then preyed on their kind hearts.
More than once this couple loaned their renters money, only
to have the renter skip town without paying back rent or
returning the money. Since the renters claimed to be
Christians, this elderly couple mistakenly trusted them.

If you fear that your elderly parents might be susceptible to
con artists, use news reports of past and current scams to
heighten their awareness and to encourage them to be wary.
Remind them not to give out their credit card numbers and to

always pay for services or purchases by check. As a safeguard, you may even want to have them call you for advice before writing checks over some specified amount, whether $50 or $500. This will enable them to retain some independence while also keeping you aware of possible problems.

What If Financial Resources Are Inadequate or Nonexistent?
Health expenses continue to escalate, in spite of managed care and other efforts to keep them under control. What if your parents do not have the financial resources to pay for care should they need it? Are you responsible to use your own resources to take care of them?

Here are some questions to consider if this is the case in your family:

1. *Can your parents sell some assets or downsize?* You may be able to increase your parents' financial resources by selling their house or other assets or by helping them downsize to a smaller home.

2. *Is living with you a viable option?* A dear friend of mine cared for her mother-in-law in her home for over twenty years while raising a large family of her own. She maintains to this day that the benefits of this arrangement were enormous to all three generations. The grandchildren got to know their grandmother as a real person, and she was always willing to baby-sit and actually helped raise her grandkids.

My friend and her husband were careful, however, to make sure Grandma did not interfere with their rules or their personal lives. Needless to say, this arrangement does not always work out well, but with some negotiation and boundary-setting, it is certainly an option.

The success you will have bringing a parent into your home to live depends on the physical and emotional health of the parent and the quality of your relationship with him or her. Sometimes having a parent live with you can work out well for a time, but as his or her health declines, the burden becomes too much to bear. If you have siblings, you may want to arrange to pool your resources so you can pay for assisted living in a quality care facility for a frail parent.

If you decide you don't have the resources to care for your parent—*don't feel guilty!* When Scripture tells us to honor our parents, it does not mean sacrificing our own financial security or that of our children.

3. What public resources are available for your parents' care? If you need financial help in caring for an aging parent, check out these resources:

- **Social Security**. Is your surviving parent getting all he or she is entitled to? For example, when a spouse dies, the surviving spouse is eligible to receive the deceased spouse's benefits. Locate Social Security offices in your local phone book.

- **Section 8 or Government Assisted Living.** The federal government subsidizes both individual homes and some nursing care. Check the Web site addresses in Appendix B as a starting point for locating information.
- **Food stamps.** Get in touch with your county welfare division for information. Food stamps are often available to people with low incomes.
- **Disability income.** Disability may be granted for either physical or mental reasons. Information is available through your local Social Security office.
- **Medicaid, Medicare, and other health insurance.** Federal health insurance is available to everyone over sixty-five, but there are many other supplemental insurance plans that help defray health care costs. Information regarding these federal insurance programs' telephone numbers can be obtained in the government section of your phone book.
- **Free or income-adjusted medical care.** Check with local teaching hospitals to determine their sliding scale fees. These hospitals should also be able to refer you to local clinics that charge fees based on income.
- **Long-term care insurance.** Available through many health insurance companies. Talk with insurance agents (preferably with your parents) about this and other options.

- **The American Association of Retired Persons** (AARP). This and other organizations provide additional insurance information for low-income elderly. (See Appendix B.)
- **The Internet.** (See Appendix B.) Many sites provide great opportunities for savings on prescription medications. Many companies also deliver health care supplies to the door.
- **Health foundations.** Foundations set up to address specific health problems (for diabetes or cancer, for instance) can be the source of answers for many questions about health-related issues. Do an Internet search or check with your doctor for information.

What About Final Expenses?

Not many people want to think about their deaths and funerals, let alone talk about or plan for them. Herb, my husband, is convinced he is going to live forever anyway, so what's the point? I have, however, reserved a plot next to my family's, and bit by bit Herb and I are talking together about funeral plans.

No matter how difficult this discussion, we strongly urge you to ask your parents—when they are still competent and able—the following questions:

- Do you want to be buried or cremated?
- Do you have a burial plot? If yes, where? If not, should one be purchased?

- Do you want a funeral or a memorial service?
- Is there anyone in particular you would like to have perform the service, if possible? Who? How can we contact that person?
- Do you have a living will? Where is it located? If not, should we draw up a living will?

It's possible to preplan cremations, casket selections, burial arrangements, and even funeral plans. Funeral homes are more than willing to discuss advance payment options, which removes a huge burden for surviving relatives at the time of death.

Granted, these are very hard topics to talk about. You want to do your best to honor your parents' final wishes, but you must know what those are. For more help in this area, see chapter nine.

If you are not able to successfully talk with your parents about these important issues, find someone they are willing to talk to—an attorney, a financial planner, even a trusted friend who can provide some direction.

Clear thinking about finances is essential for both your parents' peace of mind and your own. We want them to be financially comfortable and worry-free. Make that your goal, and make reaching it a team effort. Ask your parents to trust you enough to discuss this confidential and difficult topic now.

Chapter Four

IS YOUR DOCTOR ON SPEED DIAL?

Understanding Common Health Problems

When does a person reach old age?

My mother seemed old even in her forties. I remember her as stooped and gray-headed. Rarely active, she had little physical endurance and tended to "think old." Frail and weak, she complained chronically about various aches and pains. My older sister, on the other hand, broke her wrist when she was eighty-six and endured the pain while it healed. Now she is doing fine.

In medical school—more than a few years ago—I learned that maximum anabolism (the process by which food is changed into living tissue during metabolism) occurs in humans around age twenty! Social Security says old age starts at sixty-seven, the age we can begin drawing retirement income. But the true onset of old age can't be standardized. It depends not on how many years we've lived but how we feel physically and mentally. On the other hand, our bodies do begin to deteriorate more rapidly after we reach approximately seventy.

Following are some of the physical ailments you might expect to see in your parents as they age. We'll start with those related to the skeletal system.

Skeletal System

As a person ages, the musculoskeletal system may become stiff and uncomfortable—if not downright painful. When Herb and I go out to eat, we try hard to pretend it isn't that difficult to get up from a sitting position, but it is. We move much more slowly. Kathy finds it almost painful to watch her dad just get in and out of the car. Some of this stiffness may be due to loss of energy, as older folks tend to be less active. In addition, lower food intake and lack of important dietary elements can contribute to the deterioration of this system.

Many elderly people fall and break their hips. Everyone dreads this because broken hips can totally incapacitate people, and do not always heal well. Hip-joint replacements can restore function, but they are also risky. Mobility after such surgery can be more difficult, too. As you watch a parent struggle to rise from a chair, consider that slowness may be nature's way of protecting older folks from falls and injuries.

You can help eliminate the likelihood of a fall in several ways:
- Move your parents to a place that has no stairs.
- Eliminate clutter they might trip over.
- Make sure their living space has plenty of light. A higher

electric bill is a small price to pay to prevent this kind of injury.

- Make sure they have salt or a de-icer near all doors to the outside. Many older people fall when they first step out of the house to pick up a newspaper in inclement weather.
- Either arrange for snow and ice removal at your parents' home or do it yourself. Much like teenagers who believe nothing bad will ever happen to them, older people often tackle snow shoveling themselves. My father-in-law died of a heart attack at eighty-one while doing exactly that.

You've likely seen old people who look hunched over. This is due to a bone condition called **osteoporosis.** This condition occurs when calcium is not absorbed into bone tissue due to a decrease in sex hormones such as estrogen and testosterone. Doctors and researchers are learning more and more about osteoporosis. New medications, hormone replacement therapy for men and women, food supplements, and exercise can prevent or relieve symptoms.

If your parents are over sixty, encourage them to consult their physicians regarding bone density scans. These X-rays can detect bone deterioration early, when treatment is most effective and skeletal damage can be prevented. Without treatment, older bones fracture easily, stature diminishes, and nerves and muscles experience additional pressure.

As people age, many develop **arthritis.** The symptoms

include pain, redness, or swelling in the joints. Many treatments, particularly anti-inflammatories, can help alleviate arthritis pain. Physicians sometimes recommend physical therapy for the pain. But there is no cure and no way as yet to prevent the condition.

In general, though, the best prevention for skeletal problems of all kinds is a healthy diet, calcium supplements, hormone replacement, lots of exercise, and caution when moving around.

Digestive System

Many elderly people report that food no longer smells or tastes as good as it used to. As a result, they either eat more (hoping the food will eventually taste better), or less (because food doesn't satisfy). You can encourage your parents to better nutritional health by watching for weight gain or loss and by noting what they are eating to see how nutritious it is. Vitamins and food supplements can help balance diets, but they are no substitute for healthy eating. If your parents complain that food tastes bland, encourage them to try different seasonings and spices.

Sometimes older people eat poorly because they are unwilling or unable to spend long periods of time preparing food. To help eliminate this problem, help them find quick and simple recipes and be sure they have the ingredients in the house. If time allows, spend a day preparing and freezing meal-size portions of food for your parents. If you live away from your folks, send them care packages. You can also order groceries from Internet sites and food catalogs. If you're still worried about your parents getting enough nutrition, contact Meals on Wheels to see if they serve your parents' neighborhood.

Other digestive problems to watch for in aging parents include:

Indigestion or heartburn (gastric reflux) due to deterioration of the stomach valves, which forces food back into the esophagus. Over-the-counter antacids or medications which decrease stomach acids are very helpful.

Slowing down of the gag reflex, which can lead to blockage of the trachea by aspirated vomitus, which in turn can lead to aspiration pneumonia and possibly death. Older people should always give in to the vomiting impulse and bend over to empty the stomach rather than try to stop the vomiting.

Gall bladder problems, which can look like common indigestion. If your parent suffers from excess gas, has light-colored stools, and complains of severe pain either in the upper right abdomen or radiating from that area around the right side to the back, consult with a physician to rule out gall bladder complications. (Excess gas, by the way, can be embarrassing but is easily treated by over-the-counter or prescription drugs.)

Symptoms of stomach ulcers include dark stools and severe anemia. Ulcers may bleed internally without causing pain, so they can be overlooked. Watch for excessive fatigue that does not seem to be relieved with sleep. If you suspect an ulcer, encourage your parent to see a doctor. Ulcers can be treated with special diets, antacids, or antibiotics.

Diarrhea and **constipation** are also common digestive tract symptoms. Doctors can treat these with several different medications. These symptoms can become serious, so should be attended to if they are chronic problems.

More serious problems include **stomach and colon cancers, cancer of other organs,** and **colitis,** which is characterized by bleeding, severe constipation or diarrhea, and significant weight loss or loss of appetite. These all require immediate attention by a physician, often with subsequent surgery.

If your parents complain about digestive problems, be aware that excessive alcohol consumption exacerbates digestive problems. So can eating too late in the day.

Many medications designed to alleviate or prevent digestive symptoms, both prescription and over-the-counter, are available today. When purchasing these, always be sure the pharmacist knows what other medications your parents are taking to avoid negative drug interactions.

Cardiovascular System

Our heart and blood vessels also slow down as we get older, often resulting in some **arteriosclerosis** (hardening of the arteries), which is caused by the deposit of plaque in or on the interior walls of arteries. This plaque limits the flexibility of the artery, slows down the blood flow, and may result in blood clots or total blockage of the artery.

This circulation problem can lead to heart attacks, strokes, or pulmonary embolisms. Symptoms include numbness in various parts of the body, discoloration of the skin, and a sensation of cold. Contributing factors include excessive cholesterol and other excessive chemical build-up. If your parent has high cholesterol, he or she should be taking medication to lower it, thus helping to prevent plaque build-up in the arteries.

Elderly people should restrict their salt intake and use substitute spices to make food more appealing. They should also get moderate exercise, which will keep the heart muscle stimulated and the blood flowing more rapidly.

Because of the changes in both veins and arteries, many older people develop **high blood pressure.** Stress can exacerbate high blood pressure because it often creates tightness in the body, especially in major blood vessels. Relaxation techniques, effective problem-solving, stress reduction, diet, exercise, and medication all help reduce high blood pressure.

Myocarditis is an inflammation of the heart muscle caused

by infectious agents. Diabetics tend to be particularly susceptible to this problem. Symptoms include extreme and consistent fatigue, weakness, and low blood pressure. This disease is
progressive and potentially fatal. Heart transplants are often
the only permanent solution, although rest and treatment
with antibiotics may alleviate the symptoms.

Strokes can be caused by blood clots in the brain (which are
removed surgically) or by bleeding into the brain. A friend of
mine, Yvonne, woke in the middle of the night unable to
speak and weak on her right side. Terrified, she woke her husband, who promptly took her to the emergency room. He
knew a critical fact about strokes: if caught within the first
three hours, the recovery rate is much higher, with less permanent damage.

Blood clots commonly occur in the lower legs and can
move into the heart, lungs, or brain. Extreme cramping pain
can be symptomatic of a blood clot, particularly in the extrem-
ities, and any such pain should be examined by a physician.
Other symptoms include vomiting, nausea, severe headache,
and weakness or paralysis in any part of the body. A blood clot,
depending on where it lodges, has the potential to cause a
stroke, pulmonary embolism, or heart attack.

The elderly can have chronic **leukemia** or **anemia,** although
these diseases are generally not as fatal as they are in younger
people. Chemotherapy can help keep leukemia in check, and

anemia is often treated with iron and vitamin supplements.

It should be noted here that other chronic illnesses, **diabetes** in particular, commonly create or complicate diseases of the cardiovascular system and may impair circulation. Diabetics must address their illness with diet and medication to lower the potential of these complications. Your local Diabetes Association or hospital may offer classes to inform the public about this illness.

To help prevent cardiovascular conditions, make sure your parents are eating a healthy, low-cholesterol and low-salt diet, taking aspirin daily (to help prevent blood clots), and getting moderate exercise. Make sure they are *not* smoking. Treatment of cardiovascular problems is most effective when they are diagnosed early. Surgery or medication can correct or improve many of these conditions. Remember that too many trips to the emergency room are better than not enough.

Neurological System

Alzheimer's disease strikes fear in the hearts of many because it's progressive and so debilitating. We don't yet know the cause of this disease, although much research continues. Symptoms include a progressive loss of short-term memory, cognitive function impairment (for example, the inability to recognize familiar people or remember the date), disorientation in direction, personality changes, loss of interest in life, and emotional outbursts of sadness or anger. Eventually the person goes into a vegetative state.

Although unproven, some professionals believe that vitamin E and ibuprofen, along with consistent mental and physical activity, may help prevent or delay the onset of Alzheimer's. To date, there is no cure for the disease, although research continues on medications that could slow its progression. For more information on the effects of Alzheimer's, see chapter five.

Memory loss is not necessarily an indication of Alzheimer's. Many older folks can't remember what they had for lunch, but do remember what they wore to school on their first day of kindergarten. Several books currently in print give suggestions on improving memory at any age. (See Appendix A for a list of titles.) I have some memory loss myself and have found it helpful to attach a feeling to something I want to remember. For example, if I can feel some anxiety about remembering to bring Kathy copies of my estate plan, I am more likely to remember to do it.

A slowly progressive degeneration of the central nervous system, **Parkinson's disease** is an increasingly common disease of the elderly. Parkinson's affects 1 percent of people under sixty-five years of age (the average age of onset is about fifty-seven) and may even attack younger people. Its symptoms include slow and decreased movements, muscular rigidity, tremor of muscles even at rest, and postural instability that results in frequent falls.[1]

Medications can help control the physical limitations of Parkinson's, and there are promising surgical procedures that offer great hope for severe cases. It's important for people with this disease to remain active as long as possible. A regular exercise program and physical therapy can help patients maintain some degree of function over a longer time than they would otherwise have.

Inactivity plus the medications prescribed for this disease can result in severe constipation. A high fiber diet, stool softeners, and lots of fluids will help this problem. If you have a parent struggling with Parkinson's, the two of you might both benefit from attending a support group, available for both caregivers and victims of the disease.

Older people suffer sensory loss of all kinds, including **hearing loss**, usually due to deterioration of the auditory nerve. Loss of hearing annoys both the individual with the hearing loss and everyone around that person. People suffering from hearing loss can become irritable and blame others ("You're talking too softly"); they begin to feel isolated as well. These dynamics can affect their relationships with others.

Most hearing loss can't be cured, but hearing aids can magnify sounds and help eliminate background noise. Sometimes the elderly have trouble learning how to operate a hearing aid and eventually refuse to wear them. Do what you can to see that your parent gets proper instruction and learns how to effectively use the hearing aid.

My husband resisted wearing a hearing aid for years because he did not want to admit his impairment. Newly designed hearing aids are electronically fitted to each individual and are so small they are practically undetectable. Of course, they can also be easily lost! In addition to encouraging your parents to wear their hearing aids, work to keep background noise to a minimum and remember to speak directly to them.

Cataracts and changes in the optic nerve and retina cause **visual deterioration** in the elderly. **Glaucoma** is caused by an increase in pressure in the eyeball. It can be treated with medicated drops and at some stage may need surgical treatment. **Cataracts** need to reach a fairly serious state before surgery will be effective. Researchers continue to develop miraculous advances in eye care, including laser surgery, artificial lens implants, and retinal surgery.

Problems with balance occur as a result of neurological changes in the brain. Remind parents to slow down (but not to stop!), to be cautious in their movements, to use adequate light, and to consider using walking aids such as a cane or a walker. Make sure they are exercising whatever parts of their bodies are still usable.

One more important note: research into neurological disease has shown that older people need more physical touch to give them neurological stimulation, which helps them focus. Whenever it's possible, give your parents hugs, hold their hands, or rub their necks. Physical connections are good for you, too.

Genitourinary System

Some elderly persons report an increase in sexual problems, including **impotence** and **decreased libido**. Medication, though not without risk, can temporarily restore some sexual function for men and possibly for women. If sex is still important to a couple, drug treatment should be investigated.

Many older couples continue to enjoy sex. Even without sexual activity, however, elderly couples can enjoy intimacy. They can hold hands; hug; sit next to each other on the couch, communicating feelings as well as enjoying comfortable silences; send each other love notes; give each other back rubs. All these are satisfactory ways to meet intimacy needs.

Regular medical checkups can help catch **prostate enlargement, prostate cancer, ovarian cancer,** or **uterine cancer** in their early stages, when treatment is most effective. Elderly women continue to need annual mammograms, although the incidence of breast cancer in postmenopausal women is fairly low.

Bladder incontinence, caused by the weakening of the urethral muscles, can be embarrassing and annoying. New medications and certain surgical procedures can help strengthen these weak muscles. Urge your parents to consult a urologist for help with this annoying problem.

Other urinary tract problems include **bladder infections** (symptoms include frequent urination, burning on urinating, or blood in the urine), **kidney failure,** and **cancers of the kidneys or urinary tract.** All of these are treatable, particularly when they are caught early.

Beyond the basics of nutrition and exercise, the most important thing you can to do to help your parents maintain their health is to ensure that they see their physician on a regular basis *and* when any problem, even something that seems trivial, arises. Many stoic, older folks don't want to look foolish worrying about something minor. Often they believe minor problems will go away with time, not realizing that small problems can become big ones.

To maintain overall physical health, careful nutrition and appropriate amounts of regular exercise are essential requirements for aging bodies. Encourage your parents in these areas as much as you can.

Chapter Five

DOES THE UNDERWEAR GO ON THE INSIDE OR THE OUTSIDE?

Handling Personality Changes and Mental Deterioration

All of us change as we mature. Kathy and I certainly have! Kathy says that when she was twenty-one, she knew exactly what was right and wrong, good and bad, black and white. Today, at forty-eight, she is much less judgmental, knows much less, and is able to see opposing viewpoints. As for me, I spent a good deal of my adult life trying to please everyone and neglecting my own needs. Today, at seventy-four, I have finally decided taking care of myself is essential before I can effectively help anyone else.

Positive Changes

Many people say their parents are much better at being grand-parents than they were at being parents. Why might this be? Several reasons come to mind:

1. Grandparents usually do not spend day in and day out with their grandchildren. As my husband once told Kathy when she retrieved her son from a visit to our house: "Thanks for bringing him, and thanks for picking him up!"

2. *Grandparents are not as pressured by time constraints and demands.* I love having time to play with my younger grandchildren at whatever they want to play—without feeling guilty that the laundry isn't getting done.

3. *Grandparents have had time to develop the art of patience.* They may also be able to identify the reasons behind a grandchild's misbehavior, and help find solutions to the problem rather than simply meting out punishment.

4. *Grandparents have had time to look at their mistakes as parents.* They do not want to repeat those mistakes with their grandchildren.

5. *Grandparents do not have the pressure of feeling responsible for how grandchildren turn out.* They can enjoy time with grandkids instead of worrying about how to raise them.

Older people tend not to overwork and are often able to slow down and enjoy life more. They may have a stronger sense of humor. Kathy says that her dad is much more fun now than he ever was when she was growing up. In fact, she didn't realize until she was well into adulthood that her sense of humor had come from him.

Many mature adults, because their priorities are different than they were at an earlier age, worry less about little irritations and become less rigid and more accepting of each other.

Fran, after being married to Gerald for forty years, has given up caring that Gerald is time-challenged and always late. Now she reads a book while she waits for him to get ready, rather than harping at him to hurry. Gerald no longer mentions the ten pounds he would like Fran to lose.

Another couple I know also has learned to compromise: rather than resenting George for wanting to watch CNN twenty-four hours a day, Evelyn bought a small television for the bedroom so she can watch some of her favorite shows.

Sometimes positive changes in their parents can stir up resentment in the sandwich generation. It may be difficult to see our parents being loving and kind with their grandchildren when they were demanding, harsh, or critical with us. But as a parent yourself, you know the pressures your parents felt as they raised their family. Then as now, children don't come with instruction manuals. Our parents had only their own upbringing and Dr. Spock for guidance. They did the best they knew how.

If you understand this, you'll be better able to forgive your parents for the mistakes they made while raising you. Forgiving our parents frees us to appreciate the gifts they are giving our children. (For more about forgiveness, see chapter eight.)

Negative Changes

Sometimes personality changes in older adults are negative. Consider the following examples:

1. Loss of concern about details like housekeeping and personal appearance. Betty was an immaculate housekeeper for years. She was the only person on her block who had four children and white carpet. And it always looked white. Jealous neighbors with gray carpets speculated that Betty cleaned carpets at 3 A.M. nightly. But as Betty got older, housework became more physically demanding. Her eyesight was becoming weaker, and Betty slowly began neglecting not only the carpet, but the entire house. One of Betty's grandchildren finally noticed the state of the house when he came over to mow her lawn. Her children were able to find a housekeeper to come in every couple of weeks.

Older folks can also begin to take less interest in their personal appearance and hygiene. Sometimes this happens because they fear falling in a tub or shower. If this is the case with your parents, you can offset that fear by making their bathroom safer or by giving them a cell phone or a medical beeper for emergency use. You might also consider paying for a manicure, pedicure, haircut, or some new clothes for parents who have let their appearance go.

2. Bitterness or orneriness. Instead of mellowing and becoming nicer, some older folks become bitter or crotchety. Doug, a client of Kathy's, complained that his dad had recently developed very rigid rules about behavior in his home. A little mud on the floor from a grandchild's shoes was suddenly a huge problem. Doug couldn't understand his dad's "obsessive" behavior and had even stopped taking his three kids to see him; it only made everyone upset. Why couldn't Grandpa be reasonable?

In time Doug realized he was not going to change his dad and he needed to accept him the way he was—to give him unconditional love. Doug also found ways to live with his father's eccentricities, like inviting his dad to his house rather than taking his kids to Dad's.

If your parents make unreasonable demands, ask God to give you the patience to continue demonstrating unconditional love. Even if we disagree, we need to respect our parents' right to their own ideas and opinions, particularly if they are still living in their own homes. Doug found a good solution by moving family gatherings from his dad's home to his own.

3. Stubbornness. As older folks lose their independence (jobs, homes, decision-making), they view getting their own way as a means to personal power. Paula has been a lifetime collector of rare and beautiful things. Now in her seventies, she has become a pack rat of "potentially useful items" instead—things the rest of the family sees as junk. These items seem to provide her with a sense of security, perhaps because she grew up in the Depression and never had enough. Now she has a reserve of "stuff" she might need.

As mother and daughter, Kathy and I can tell you firsthand that pack rats can develop conflicts with spouses who are not pack rats, or adult children who want to clean up their "stuff." Kathy is fairly certain that she will have to rent a dumpster when she has to clean out Herb's and my house, but she says that's easier than getting either of us to throw anything away! We recommend that once you have talked to your parents about downsizing and they've made it clear they aren't interested—let them be (other than checking for safety). It simply isn't worth the stress that fighting about it puts on you and your relationship with them.

4. Withdrawal. Older persons can start to withdraw from others, particularly from folks their own age. William, age seventy, was constantly asked to join the active senior citizen group at his church. He didn't want to participate because he didn't want to be around "all those old people." William and his wife, Donna, found themselves more and more content to vegetate at home. Then Tony and Lynn, a fifty-something couple from the church, developed a real friendship with William and Donna and began to spend some time with them. Both couples enjoy their intergenerational friendship. It is important for people like William to develop relationships with people of differing ages.

Lindsey is the young mother of two toddlers. Every couple of weeks, she calls Wilma, a seventy-one-year-old widow who lives in her neighborhood, and invites her for coffee and child-rearing advice. Wilma is the mother of five successful adult children and grandmother of eight terrific grandkids, but Lindsey's friendship makes her feel needed and valued in a special way. For her part, Lindsey feels loved and benefits from Wilma's wisdom.

Dementia and Alzheimer's

In the previous chapter we briefly discussed neurological changes that occur in the elderly. While those changes are of a physical nature, they produce distressing changes in thinking and behavior. Mental problems in this age group are, unfortunately, common and debilitating.

Dementia is a chronic deterioration of intellectual function and other cognitive skills, severe enough to interfere with normal activities of daily life. It may begin at any age, but it is primarily a disease of the elderly. It affects 15 percent of people over sixty-five, and up to 40 percent of those over eighty.[1] It may be related to Alzheimer's disease, but there are at least thirty-five other causes of dementia as well. These include injuries, infections, metabolic abnormalities, degenerative diseases, anemia, viral infections, and long-term alcohol abuse.

Sadly, there is no cure for this frustrating and debilitating state. However, many types of dementia respond to early intervention, so be sure to check with a physician at the first signs in your parents of forgetfulness or failure to recognize common objects.

The other most common illness that affects intellectual function is **Alzheimer's disease**. During the late stages of my own father's Alzheimer's, I gained many insights about this illness. At age seventy-two, he began to wander away from the home where he had lived and raised his family for forty years. Fortunately, this was a close-knit rural community, so a kind neighbor would always bring him home safely. One day I asked Dad, "When you leave here, where are you going?"

Dad replied promptly, "I'm trying to find my home!" To me, the house where I had grown up had always been "home," but instead of arguing the point, I asked, "Do you mean the home where you grew up, Dad?"

With immense relief and a few rarely shed tears, Dad nodded. "I get so homesick for my home!" That home was some five miles away, and he could not have found it. Even a visit there satisfied his yearning only temporarily, if at all. But this conversation gave me understanding.

Time Magazine recently ran a cover story on Alzheimer's disease. The author estimated that twenty million people suffer from this illness worldwide—four million in the United States—and that those numbers could triple by the year 2050.

While this disease primarily strikes elderly people, early onset cases can occur, though rarely, even in the thirties. Research on Alzheimer's is currently two-pronged, focusing both on how genetics contributes to one's susceptibility to the disease and how environmental factors figure into the problem.[2]

Radical personality changes can indicate the onset of this horrible illness. My father, one of the kindest, most humorous and delightful people I ever knew, became morose and withdrawn and at the slightest provocation even violent, hitting both his physician and his caretakers.

Max, on the other hand, had "raised swearing to an art form" in his adult life, in the words of his kids and grandkids. But after his Alzheimer's became severe, Max completely stopped swearing. When his son asked him why he didn't swear anymore, Max replied, "I don't know what you mean. I've never sworn in my life!"

Some Alzheimer's patients become exhibitionistic. This was the case with Jared, whose wife had placed him in a care center because of the severity of his Alzheimer's. Jared loved nothing more than "flashing" himself whenever a female nurse walked into his room. Talks from his family and the care center administrators did absolutely no good, as Jared was not even aware he was doing this, and denied it when confronted. Fortunately, most of the nurses had good senses of humor and learned to expect this behavior.

Alzheimer's has three distinct stages with escalating symptoms:

Stage One: Mild (Two to four years' duration)

- Increased forgetfulness that interferes with ability to hold a job or complete household tasks
- Forgets names for simple things like bread or butter
- Has trouble recognizing what numbers mean
- Loses initiative and interest in favorite activities or hobbies
- Decreased judgment that leads to, for example, wearing a bathrobe to the park

Stage Two: Moderate (Two to eight years' duration)

- Unable to recognize close friends and family
- Wanders about, gets lost
- Increased confusion, anxiety, and personality changes
- Forgets how to complete common daily tasks like getting dressed or brushing teeth
- Delusions
- Insomnia

Stage Three: Severe (One to three years' duration)

- Unable to remember anything or process new information, can't recognize family
- Can't use or understand words but still responds to music, touch, or eye contact
- Difficulty eating, swallowing
- Unable to dress, bathe, or groom self; unable to control bladder and bowel function
- Bedridden[3]

Generally, in Stage One, with adequate support, an Alzheimer's patient can still live at home. By Stage Two, independent living becomes increasingly risky. By Stage Three, the patient needs to be placed in residential care.

Research indicates that even when people no longer recognize family members, they are aware of a loving presence. If your parents have dementia or Alzheimer's, spend time with them. Don't contradict them or tell them they are not remembering things correctly. Instead, listen to their tales of childhood, find old photographs, or, if possible, physically take them to the places of their own childhood. Sharing memories and reliving yesteryears can be comforting to people in the early stages of dementia.

Listening carefully is critical—many of us get impatient with older people who "ramble," but if I had not listened to Dad's answer to my question about where he was going when he wandered away from home, I might never have realized what he was feeling.

Medical breakthroughs continue to occur with regard to Alzheimer's and dementia. But for now, accepting our parents unconditionally means accepting them as they are today. Positive changes in our parents certainly are easier to accept than negative ones. We may have to set some limits with our parents when changes get too negative, but we can certainly still love them. We must not physically abandon them, no matter how difficult it might be to see their mental deterioration. Keep in mind how you want your children to treat you when you are no longer able to care for yourself, and treat your parents accordingly.

One final note: if you are caring for an elderly parent who suffers from Alzheimer's or dementia, please remember to take care of yourself as well. (See chapter ten). As I have learned, if you don't take care of yourself, you can't take care of anyone else.

Chapter Six

HOME MAY NOT BE WHERE THE HEART IS

Weighing Alternatives for Assisted Living

Mary Louise's mother had multiple sclerosis for years and managed to cope just fine. But the disease progressed, and by her late sixties, confined to a wheelchair, she was often in the hospital for heart failure and other physical ailments.

Mary Louise did not realize how serious her mother's health problems were until a visit from out of town after her mother's most recent release from the hospital. She walked into her mother's room directly from the airport to discover that the older woman had had an attack of diarrhea and was unable to clean the mess herself. Mary Louise, already tired from a six-hour flight, helped her into the bathtub, washed the linens, and then helped her into clean clothes and back into bed.

Her mother had always said that she didn't want to go to an "old folks home"—but Mary Louise had suddenly become very concerned about her mother's ability to live alone. What should she do?

Telltale Signs

There may come a time when you are faced with a similar decision. How do you know when your parents should no longer live without some level of assistance? Here are some signs that intervention may be needed:

1. A life- or health-threatening living environment. This might include unsanitary conditions around the house (bugs, mice, or unclean toilets, for example), property damage that goes unnoticed or unrepaired, broken locks, or evidence of kitchen fires from neglect while cooking. Because the environment tends to slip a little at a time, older people can be unaware of the actual condition of their homes.

2. Unwillingness to accept help. Do your parents refuse to allow strangers in the house to help with housework or personal care? In some cases such obstinacy can endanger their health. After eighty-four-year-old Nona suffered a stroke, her doctor and family made arrangements for a physical therapist to come to her home each week to teach her how to use a walker to increase her mobility. After a week or so, she told the physical therapist not to come back: "You aren't doing anything to help me! This is stupid!" Nothing her children or doctor said could convince her or her husband otherwise.

3. Physical incapacity that makes self-care difficult or impossible. Mary Louise's mother was unable to clean up after herself when she suffered diarrhea. If Mary Louise hadn't arrived, who knows how long her mother would have sat in the mess? Dorothy and Bill provide another example. Married for over fifty years when Bill was diagnosed with Parkinson's disease, the couple continued living at home, where Dorothy cared for him. But over the years his physical needs have increased to the point that she is no longer able to help him. Aging herself, Dorothy isn't strong enough to lift Bill in and out of bed or help him up when he falls.

4. Inability to take responsibility for finances. Parents who are unable or unwilling to balance checkbooks, remember details of bill paying, or keep track of accounts become easy targets of con artists and may not be able to continue living independently.

5. Mental deterioration leading to dangerous situations. Simon began to wander away from his home and get lost. His neighbors were good about watching out for him, but they weren't always home or looking out the window when he left his house. What happens when Simon ends up in a place where no one knows him and he can't find his way home?

After her husband died, Ellen became disoriented, confused, and hostile. She even hit her son as he was trying to calm her down. No amount of talking helped, and it became clear that Ellen was no longer the practical, rational woman she had been.

If you recognize any of these symptoms in your parents, talk with them about your concerns. See if they are open to getting the help they need, whether that means having someone come in to cook and clean or moving to a place where they can receive the level of care they require. Do this in as kindly and empathic a manner as possible.

What If They Refuse Help?

Here is a worst-case scenario. Robert, who is in his mid-eighties, and Joan, who is in her late seventies, have been married for sixty years—and can't stand each other. Joan has a life-threatening illness that requires frequent trips to doctors and hospitals and prevents her from physically being able to keep up the house or prepare meals. Yet Robert still expects her to wait on him hand and foot, refuses to acknowledge her physical limitations, and offers no help.

When their son, Matt, came for a visit to check in on them, he found the house and yard a filthy shambles, both parents miserable, and Robert unwilling to change anything. Both his parents refused to ask for any outside help, let alone accept it.

Matt lives over three hundred miles away. His sister, when Matt asked her to help him talk with their parents, told him that God would provide for them. (In other words, she didn't want anything to do with the situation.) What should Matt do? Should he allow his parents to remain at home, even though that might be dangerous, or should he risk forcing a move that might leave them hateful or resentful toward him?

There are several courses of action Matt can take at this point. One, he can clean up the house and yard, even if his parents don't like it. Of course, this will be only a temporary remedy, as the problem will arise again unless he is able to convince his parents they cannot maintain their home as they have in the past.

Two, he can see his mother's physician for information about her prognosis and what to expect in terms of her physical needs, and for recommendations for her ongoing care.

Three, he can find outside help to assist his parents at home on a regular basis: other relatives, neighbors, church members, professionals. But he will have to convince his parents to let these people into their home to help.

Four, he can meet with a legal advisor or lawyer to get Robert and Joan declared incompetent and become their legal guardian. This is a heartbreaking, costly decision, both financially and emotionally. (If you are not sure how this process works in your state, check with your Division of Aging. Typically, two doctors who do not collaborate must examine the patient's mental state and determine by some acceptable, objective criteria that a person is not capable to make crucial decisions.) If the doctors deem Matt's parents not capable, a legal advisor or lawyer can prepare a power of attorney certificate that will allow Matt to make financial and placement decisions for his parents.

The best scenario would be for Matt and his sister to agree on this course of action, but if his sister is unwilling to get involved, Matt alone can begin the process of scheduling evaluations and pursuing legalities. If his parents refuse the evaluation, the court can insist on their cooperation. If his sister disagrees with the eventual judgment, she may either agree to take over responsibility for their parents, or she will be forced to comply with the judgment of the court.

What should Matt do? What should *you* do if faced with a similar decision?

The two of us can't make this decision for you or for anyone else. If you find yourself in this hard place, pray for wisdom and seek the counsel of family members and medical professionals. Whatever you decide, you must not let anyone else criticize or second-guess your decision. *Do not feel guilty about your decision!*

If you decide to move your parent or parents to a facility where they can get help, expect them to be angry, frustrated, and even hostile. None of us like it when we have to do things we don't want to do. Doing the best thing for our parents—much like doing the best thing for our children—does not always mean doing the popular thing or the thing they would like.

Show compassion for what they are going through. In similar circumstances, you would likely feel angry, too. Allow your parents to express their negative feelings. Validate those feelings. Tell them that you wish things did not have to be this way. Try your hardest not to react to their anger; you will only intensify it.

Try also to get them to focus on the positives in their lives: the children and grandchildren who love them, the contributions they have made, the contributions they still have to make. Give them things to look forward to—visits with the family at holidays, birthday celebrations, perhaps attendance at sports and school events to watch the grandchildren perform.

Above all, *do not allow your parents' anger to make you feel guilty!* Remember all the decisions you had to make for your children when they were small? The ones they didn't like but you did for their good? When your parents aren't competent to make their own decisions, you must do what's best for them even if they don't like it.

Once the decision is made to move your parents out of their own home, you'll need to decide on the best alternative living arrangement. Start with your state Division of Aging (check the government listings in your phone book). This agency provides personnel to visit elderly folks in their homes to assess the severity of the living situation and to make recommendations for alternative care.

Alternative Living Arrangements

Alternative living arrangements range from moving your parents into your home to placing them in foster care to placing them in a facility with progressive levels of care. These are your options:

1. Move your parent(s) into your own home. We know several families who have modified or added on to their houses to provide privacy and space for their parents. Even if you can't modify your home, you may be able to move a parent into an extra bedroom. In order for this arrangement to work on a long-term basis, of course, you and your family must be on relatively good terms with your parents! Everyone needs to be flexible and able to compromise and negotiate.

2. Retirement centers. Most adult care facilities offer three progressive levels of care: independent, assisted living, and nursing care. Many provide apartments for independent living with on-call help and transportation for grocery shopping and doctor visits as needed. If keeping up the apartment gets to be too demanding, a person or couple can move to the assisted living section of the facility, which offers a single room, three meals a day in a dining room, and housecleaning every two weeks. When and if a resident becomes bedridden or is unable to attend to personal hygiene or take medication properly, he or she can be moved to the nursing home section to receive skilled nursing care.

In addition, many assisted living facilities offer special care for special needs. For example, *acute care* might be provided for crisis or temporary situations such as broken bones or stroke recovery. *Intermediate care* might provide physical therapy and other rehabilitation services to assist in recovery from physical problems which can be improved. *Long-term* or *custodial care* might be provided for residents with chronic problems such as Alzheimer's or Parkinson's disease.

Making a Decision

How do you decide which care facility is best for your parents' needs? Consider the following:

1. Ask for recommendations from friends. Check out these facilities first.

2. Determine what you or your parents can afford. David and his brothers were concerned about how they would pay for their mother's care. They knew she needed skilled nursing care, but the cost was so high they could not afford it. Then someone encouraged David to look into Medicaid. If his mother was eligible, Medicaid would cover all the costs incurred from her care that she was unable to pay herself—including medication, housing costs, and hospital and medical costs.

If your parents' income is low, they may be eligible for **Medicaid**, which is both federally and state funded. The programs vary from state to state, but generally private insurance carriers will pay for long-term care for some specific period of time. When all other insurance options are exhausted, Medicaid is the final resort. To research this further, look in the phone book under federal government agencies. Not all facilities take Medicaid patients, so when you're doing your research on specific care centers, be sure to ask.

In addition, many health-care companies provide policies that cover long-term care. The premium for this service is not usually included in regular premium payments. Check with your parents' insurance agent, and if long-term care is not covered, call other insurance companies to investigate the cost and benefits.

3. Visit several retirement facilities before you make a selection. When you visit retirement centers, go first to the nursing home section and smell it. Need we say more? Keep in mind, of course, that many elderly people refuse assistance for baths.

Look at the posture of folks in wheelchairs. Are the chairs adjusted so people are comfortable and upright? Be aware of the atmosphere of the facility. Does it seem gloomy? Are people (residents and staff) smiling? Are there plants? Do residents look well-groomed? Are residents encouraged to help themselves as much as possible? Is there an activities program?

Visit with and listen to residents, if possible. Have a meal and check out the food quality, choice, and amount. Is the dining room pleasant? Insist on seeing every part of the facility, including the kitchen and laundry. Drop in at unexpected times. (Remember when you did that for your child's pre-school?)

Once your parents are in a facility, visit them at least weekly. Take them out if they are physically able. Eat a meal with them in the dining room. Encourage other friends, relatives, and clergy to visit them. Try to get them interested in reading material, television, or music. Encourage some kind of hobby. Such stimulation helps keep older people focused and aware. If you live too far away for weekly visits, send cards and letters or make regular phone calls.

The decision to place an elderly parent in a care center is one of the most difficult decisions in life. Nevertheless, it may be a lifesaver for both you and your parents.

Chapter Seven

WHEN THE ANSWER TO YOUR PRAYER
IS NOT THE ONE YOU WANTED
Dealing With Spiritual Issues

Sam lost his beloved wife after forty-eight years of marriage. His kids were grown and doing well, but he desperately missed Rachel. He had prayed consistently for her healing, and when she died, he felt God had deserted him. He was angry at God and even questioned God's existence.

Sam's oldest son, John, repeatedly reminded Sam of all the times in his life when God had answered his prayers positively. John reminded his father of God's gifts to him (a loving family, wonderful memories of Rachel), and shared with Sam his own faith. Sam's grandson, Jason, also told his grandfather about a time when he prayed for something and God said, "No." Fortunately, Sam was able to restore his faith in God and come to accept his loss.

Helping Parents Who Are Spiritually Struggling

A relationship with God can give us comfort in loss, strength to persevere in difficult times, and hope for the future. If our parents have a vital, vibrant relationship with God, it can sustain them through the many losses they are facing as they age.

Some older people develop an apathy or a complacency toward matters of faith. Perhaps they begin to take their spiritual life for granted and forget that it needs attention. Perhaps they begin to feel ill or weak and getting up to go to church is too much effort. Perhaps they begin to feel discounted or uncomfortable in a church geared more to young people than older members.

I understand this feeling firsthand. My husband and I are charter members of our church; we have been active there for fifty years. We have served on the church board, and Herb has been the church chairman. But the Sunday morning church service and music have changed so much that we no longer feel at home there. It's tempting to leave and not even bother to find another place to worship, but we have chosen to stay. It helps that my youngest daughter and her family now attend this church.

Churches and synagogues need to develop stronger ministries for the elderly. If you are part of the sandwich generation, you might pray about being involved in addressing this need in your own church. The elderly need programs and support systems just as much as new moms or young married couples do. And they need to be made to feel that they have something vital to offer the church.

Vera, age seventy-eight, had taught public school and Sunday school for five decades. She heard that the Vacation Bible School at her church needed volunteers, so she immediately offered her services. Her church turned her down, with no good explanation. What a waste of resources! And what a rejection of the concept of God's unconditional acceptance! You can be a part of changing these attitudes—and maybe by the time you are seventy-eight, the attitude in the church will be more positive toward the elderly.

The rejection Vera experienced is just the kind of thing that can turn a heart away from God. Another source of anger and bitterness toward God is apparently unanswered prayer. That was true for Deborah's eighty-six-year-old grandmother, Millie. Millie was dying of cancer and in a great deal of pain. She felt extremely bitter and angry at God, and was vocal about expressing her feelings.

"But Grandma," Deborah reminded her, "what about Jesus? You've served him all your life." That was true; Millie had struggled to maintain her faith throughout a very hard life. But now she was in severe pain and knew she was dying. She needed someone to blame, and so she blamed God. "Jesus?" she said to Deborah. "What's he ever done for me?"

Millie's honesty about her anger gave her family an opportunity to remind her of the many times Jesus had walked with her through difficulties. After repeatedly being reminded of the things God had done for their family, she finally acknowledged, "You're right. I guess I have to trust God."

How we see God influences our faith. A Jewish rabbi once told me that his religion teaches him to ask God for strength to deal with life's trials, instead of using God as our "order taker" to give us everything we ask for and make our lives easy. When our children are mad at us, they often say things like, "I wish I had Susie's mommy." We accept their feelings, know that they don't mean it, and are not threatened by their anger. In fact, we explore their anger with them and help them find solutions.

We need to do the same with our parents when they feel angry at God. Help them acknowledge their anger. Remind them that God doesn't abandon his children, even when we push him away. Let them talk about their feelings. Remind them who God is. If we do these things rather than feel threatened by their feelings, we may be able to help them move through their anger into acceptance of God's will.

Even if your parents are spiritually vibrant, you should accompany them to church (or have them accompany you), talk with them about spiritual things, encourage them to share their faith, and remind them of the ways God has worked in their lives and in yours. Hebrews 11 and 12, in which Paul recounts the many miracles God worked in the Old Testament, encourages us to remember miracles in our own lives.

What If Your Parents Have No Faith?

We don't all have the privilege of sharing a common faith with our parents. Whether you agree with your parents' beliefs or not, never criticize or argue with them in a way that demeans or alienates them. One thing you positively must do is pray. Prayer is a powerful tool in helping others discover faith.

Talk to your parents about your own faith and how you see God acting in your life. Encourage them to read about some of the recent studies that emphasize the value of spirituality and prayer in physical healing. You might also have a tactful, thoughtful, and nonjudgmental clergyman or church member visit your parents. Finding someone who is willing to develop a long-term friendship with them would be even better. Avoid anyone who appears harsh or critical, or who might resemble someone your parents had conflicts with in their childhood churches.

Frank had been raised in a strict, legalistic Protestant denomination. He hated going to church as a child. The minister in his church preached hellfire and brimstone and frightened Frank. There was a period of twenty years as an adult when he rarely, if ever, attended church, although his wife and children did.

After his parents died, he finally felt free to explore other churches. At age sixty-two, he discovered a church where he felt comfortable and accepted. He began reading his Bible, became active in the church, and developed a true friendship with the minister. In fact, Frank felt so comfortable with this man that when he felt the pastor had strayed from biblical teaching, he was able to talk with him about his concerns. Frank rediscovered faith late in his life, primarily through the intervention of this kind and open minister.

If none of your attempts seem to bring your parents to faith, remember that only God knows a person's heart. And don't give up on the things you *can* do:

- Continue to show your parents unconditional love.
- Create a spiritual, peaceful atmosphere in your home when they visit.
- Pray for them and ask others for their prayers.

Remember—God cares for your parents even more than you do!

Chapter Eight

TO ERR IS HUMAN; TO FORGIVE IS DIFFICULT ...
AND DIVINE

Forgiving the Hurts of the Past

You may have conflicting feelings about helping your elderly parents. Perhaps they were not nurturing and loving to you when you were a child; perhaps they abandoned you or even abused you. But now your parents are getting old. They may be sick and need help. You feel torn about what to do. You want to help, but you don't want to help. You resent even being asked. If this describes you, we urge you to forgive your parents.

Holly's Story

Holly grew up with a rigid, stern, emotionally absent father. Her mother, intimidated herself by her husband's temper, didn't intervene. Holly dreamed of having her own children, and hoped against hope that her dad would love them and show them the kindness he had not given her.

Eventually Holly moved hundreds of miles away and married Kevin. They had two great kids. When the children were four and two years of age, Holly's parents finally came to visit for a few weeks. Holly was horrified to see that instead of mellowing with age, her dad had become even more irascible and rigid. This was especially disturbing because he was so harsh with her children. He told Holly she was not being strict enough with them, and reminded her that he had been very strict with her and that she had turned out all right.

When the disastrous visit ended, Holly was happy to see her parents leave. She felt guilty, though. She also felt extremely disappointed as she acknowledged that her dad would never be the loving grandfather she had always wanted for her kids. In fact, she felt she had to protect her children from him.

Her dad's visit also brought up Holly's own grief over not having had a loving father. She became so depressed that Kevin suggested she talk to a professional. When she came to see me, she was full of conflicted feelings and resentments and she doubted that she was a good mom, in spite of Kevin's constant reassurance. In her heart, Holly had always believed that her dad had been so harsh with her because she had been such a bad child.

I asked her to find out as much as she could about how her dad had grown up, something he had never talked about with her. She talked to her mother and her dad's two sisters, and gradually developed a picture of her father's childhood. Holly's grandfather had been even harsher and more rigid than her dad, beating him often with a leather razor strop. He did not believe boys should show their feelings—except for anger. Anger alone went unpunished.

Holly's mother told her that her father always believed his dad treated him harshly because he deserved it. He had also convinced himself that his success in business was due to his severe upbringing. Once he had convinced himself that his own upbringing had been good for him, he repeated the pattern of mistreatment with his daughter and then with his grandchildren.

As Holly gained perspective, she began to see that she had not been a terrible child; her father treated her harshly because he himself had been treated harshly and his wounded heart had never healed. Once she realized that her dad was a victim of his own childhood, she was able to forgive him. She told him something like this:

"Dad, I finally understand why you are who you are and why I have resented you. I know you wanted the best for me, but your methods were often too harsh. Seeing you with Tiffany and Justin brought this all back to me. I know you don't think you did anything wrong, but my feelings were often very hurt as a child, and sometimes I still feel hurt.

"I have forgiven you and love you because you're my dad. I

want you and Mom to visit often and to spend time with Tiffany and Justin, but there will have to be one or two rules. It is up to Kevin and me to discipline them. I want them to have fabulous memories of a kind, fun, loving grandfather. And I want you to enjoy spoiling them and playing with them, but not have to worry about them—that is the job of their parents."

Fortunately, Holly's dad changed. But even if he hadn't, Holly had learned some valuable insights. She learned that she was neither a bad child nor a bad parent, and she learned that with God's grace she could forgive her dad. Forgiving him led to great freedom. Her dad could no longer hurt her feelings.

Emotional Distance

Holly felt emotionally distant from her father because of his abuse, but abuse isn't the only cause of emotional distance. When families are so busy they don't spend quiet time together, the children's primary emotional experiences take place with others. Adult children who were "parked" with caretakers while growing up may tend to park their elderly parents in nursing facilities and abandon them. If we do not close the emotional gaps between ourselves and our parents—if we don't forgive them—we may come to regret it after they die.

If your parents have been emotionally distant from you, here are some things you can do:

1. Try to understand how your parents got to be who they are. Their own childhood experiences and belief systems may have led them to make mistakes or errors in spite of good intentions. Most parents truly love their children and want the best for them; they do not hurt children intentionally.

2. Accept the differences between you and your parents (accepting them does not mean liking or agreeing with those differences). My mom, a devout Nazarene, sincerely believed that everyone who was not a perfect Christian was going to hell. It certainly was not my job to convince her otherwise. My job was to love her unconditionally.

3. Apologize for your own mistakes or stubbornness without expecting an apology in return. Sometimes parents are looking for an opening to make their own apologies, but we can't count on that.

4. Share hurt feelings and ask for what you need. "I felt so hurt when you did this, and I would like you to apologize." Again, don't expect a specific response. Just saying this can keep us from blaming our parents and using hurtful experiences to stay angry.

5. Be willing to close the distance and initiate closeness even if your parents don't know how. Appreciate them, show interest in their lives, express affection, and stay in touch, regardless of their response. In other words, do it because it frees you and it creates the best possible climate for them to eventually come to their senses.

6. Forgive your parents for not being perfect—for being human and making mistakes. Sometimes you need to forgive even when they have not apologized.

What It Means to Forgive

Forgiveness is not excusing or condoning wrong behavior. It is not superficial or temporary. It is not easy. And it is not necessarily for the other person's benefit.

There is an old axiom about "forgiving and forgetting." Forgetting is not possible, nor is it especially desirable. We need to remember the lessons we've learned. But it is possible to put a hurtful incident or event in a closet in our minds and not bring it out again. When we continue to bring up the past, we keep everyone trapped there. It starts to feel as if we can't change anything for the future.

How do we let go of the past? Here are five steps to forgiveness:

1. Instead of trying to convince yourself that you don't care, acknowledge the pain you have suffered.

2. Get information. Find out how the person who hurt you got to be who he or she is. What was behind his or her hurtful behavior?

3. Be willing to turn that information into understanding of the person who hurt you.

4. Make a conscious choice to let understanding lead to forgiveness.

5. Set boundaries. Do not continue to accept hurtful behaviors. For example, if a parent becomes critical on the phone, say you have to go and will talk with them later.

Both Kathy and I have counseled many people who have lifelong regrets for not making an opportunity to reconcile with their parents. Attempting to reconcile, even if our parents are unwilling to reciprocate, replaces regret with peace—and offers parents the best possible climate in which to ask for or grant their own forgiveness.

What Happens When We Forgive Our Parents?
Forgiveness is powerful and beneficial. When we forgive someone for hurting us, it frees us from feeling like victims or feeling we are under the power of the person who hurt us. Without forgiveness, we often continue to feel helpless and at the mercy of whoever is hurting us. Forgiveness frees us from a deep-seated belief that we are the "bad guy" and gives us an opportunity to choose our responses to hurtful people.

Forgiveness can free the perpetrator as well as the victim of hurtful behavior. Lydia, depressed because of her own bad experiences as a child, had been cold and withdrawn as a mom. Her daughter, Nicole, spent most of her childhood feeling hurt and resentful that Lydia was not like her friends' moms. She missed having a mother who would have tea parties with her! When Nicole finally had children of her own, she began to understand the demands and pressures of parenthood, and eventually was able to tell her mother that she forgave her for her mistakes. When she did, Lydia broke down in tears, telling her daughter she had always known she needed forgiveness but hadn't known how to ask.

Forgiveness enables us to set boundaries not out of anger or fear but out of the strength of what we know to be right. Holly needed to protect Tiffany and Justin from an angry grandfather, but she was able to do it lovingly and without trying to retaliate against her dad.

Forgiveness allows us to feel like equal adults with our parents. Many of Kathy's clients say that when they go home to visit their parents, they feel like children again. Once we have forgiven our parents, we assume a new position in relation to them—one of independence, self-respect, and equality.

Forgiveness provides the maximum possibility for reconciliation. If we don't forgive, we stay stuck in anger and bitterness. Forgiveness alone doesn't *promise* reconciliation, which takes equal effort on the parts of both parent and child. But it breaks down emotional walls and helps us come to the point where we can offer grace.

Barry and his father had a serious, damaging disagreement.

Barry was later able to forgive his dad and tried to reestablish a good relationship with him, but his father, believing that forgiving Barry would mean giving in, refused to do so.

Barry continued to send his dad cards for Christmas, Father's Day, and other occasions, and often called to talk. Although his dad never responded, Barry felt he had done all he could and was continuing to do the right thing by trying to reestablish the relationship. He was able to define the relationship without expectations of receiving something in return.

Forgiveness is a process, a decision that frees us from bitterness and misery. "If you forgive men their trespasses, your heavenly Father also will forgive you," Matthew 6:14-15 (RSV) reminds us. "But if you do not forgive men their trespasses, neither will your Father forgive your trespasses."

Forgive your parents. No matter how they respond, you'll find peace—and forgiveness for your own shortcomings.

Chapter Nine

IT'S MY PARTY, I CAN DIE IF I WANT TO

Coming to Terms With Death and Dying

We have seen a huge media campaign in the last few years addressing the topic of dying. PBS recently broadcast a four part series called "On Our Own Terms: Moyers on Dying." *Modern Maturity* reviewed the series and further addressed issues of aging and dying in modern America, and *Time Magazine* made "Dying on Our Own Terms" its cover story shortly thereafter.

In the *Modern Maturity* article mentioned above, Bill Moyers revealed that he and his wife had created the PBS series on dying because their son had started thinking about his parents' deaths. Our society has not done a good job of taking care of people as they die, Moyers believes—and we are finally realizing it.[1]

Most Americans don't think of death in the same way we think of birth—that is, that it is a natural part of life. This hasn't always been the case, however. Many people in my generation remember being present when a loved one died; they were connected to the process of death and were not afraid of it. Today, clergymen and even doctors are often uncomfortable discussing details of dying and have received very little, if any, training in helping others cope with the end of life.

In our research for this book, we uncovered some other interesting facts:

- In a Time/CNN poll, seven out of ten Americans polled said they would rather die at home than in hospitals—yet 75 percent die in health care facilities rather than at home.[2]

- Most people want to be aware of the experience of dying. They do not want to be overly medicated, but they do want their pain controlled. Yet nearly half of dying Americans exit their lives in pain while being attended to by strangers.[3]

- Many dying people are not depressed, but rather seem to adapt to the process of death. My sister-in-law, who had been diagnosed with cancer for over a year, told me that she often prayed for death—not because she was morbid, but because she was ready for it.

Our goal for our parents should be to maintain the highest possible quality of life for them for as long as possible. Yes, it's difficult to talk with your parents about death and dying. But if you address these issues when your mom and dad are still healthy, it will help ease the stress when the end of their lives draw near.

Talk With Parents About Their Wishes

In order to prepare yourself and your parents for their inevitable death, we encourage you to discuss Jim Towey's "Five Wishes" with them. Towey, an attorney, is the founder of an organization called Aging With Dignity. Here are the questions he urges every aging person to consider:

1. Who do I want to make care decisions for me when I can't?

2. What kind of medical treatment do I want toward the end?

3. What would help me feel comfortable while I am dying?

4. How do I want people to treat me?

5. What do I want my loved ones to know about me and my feelings after I'm gone?[4]

Once you have talked with parents about these issues, you need to be sure they have an advance directive. There are two types of advance directives:

- *Living Wills.* A Living Will details what kind of life-sustaining treatment a person wants or doesn't want when death is imminent.

- *Durable Power of Attorney.* A durable power of attorney appoints someone to be a person's decision maker if that person can't speak for him- or herself. The person appointed is also called a "surrogate," "attorney-in-fact," or "health-care proxy."

Make Sure Doctors Do All They Can

Make sure your parents' primary care physician understands the special health needs of the elderly and gives treatment as needed. You might be surprised to learn that not all doctors feel the elderly should receive treatment. When eighty-year-old Shirley's doctor didn't request that she get a mammogram that year, she asked him about it. His reply? "You have to die sometime. Besides, mammograms don't cure cancer." That was the last time she saw that doctor!

Spencer's primary care physician told him he had testicular cancer, but it was too advanced for treatment—and at seventy-nine, he was too old for treatment! Spencer had recently remarried after the death of his first wife and was extremely active and vital. Rather than giving up and accepting the doctor's verdict, he pursued several other oncology specialists until he did receive treatment. His cancer went into remission.

Your Parent Need Not Suffer Pain

If your parent is in pain and does not have a doctor who prescribes medication to alleviate it, find a doctor who will. Too often, elderly people accept the diagnosis and treatment of their family or primary care physicians, even when the treatment does not eliminate pain or reduce symptoms.

One reason this happens is the expense of seeing another doctor when insurance may not provide for a second opinion. If cost is truly a problem, most communities have tax-supported hospitals that provide services at a reduced cost. Remember, too, that while second opinions may cost more initially, they can save a great deal of money in the long run.

Kathy and I often hear stories of dying people suffering incredible amounts of pain because physicians do not want to "overmedicate" them or prescribe "addicting" drugs. Yet hospitals are now required to develop plans for pain management. So ask for a second opinion—or a third or a fourth. It is extremely rare that terminally ill people become addicted to any type of pain medication.

An old family friend of ours was diagnosed with bone cancer, which is very painful. In order to allow her to be at home, her doctor gave her intravenous equipment so she could administer her own pain medication. This device enabled her to live comfortably, enjoy her friends, and stay independent until just a week prior to her death—at home, with hospice care, as she had requested. She never displayed any signs of addiction, and her quality of life was greatly enhanced by the medications.

If You Know They Are Dying

If your parent is diagnosed with a terminal illness, consider whether hospice care (available *only* for those with a terminal illness) is an option. Before a person can receive hospice care, he or she has to stop all life-prolonging treatments. Hospice workers then attempt to help the patient and the family comfort each other in accepting death.

Hospice workers are experts on death and dying. They are willing to talk with family members about any and all concerns regarding the death of a loved one. Also called "palliative care," hospice emphasizes physical, spiritual, and emotional comfort during the dying process and is now considered a sub-specialty in medicine. Health insurance or Medicare usually covers the cost of hospice care.

In recent years, hospice care has enabled people to be with their loved ones as they are dying. Some hospices are separate entities, but most provide in-home care. Nurses and other professionals check on patients and their families on a regular basis. They also let families know when the patient needs extra help or when caregivers need breaks. Hospice services may also include respite care, medication management, and assistance from counselors, home-care aides, and grief specialists.

When medication and surgery had finally run their course, Leon accepted that his heart condition was terminal. He asked his family to get a hospice involved. Nurses and counselors came by the house almost daily. One counselor in particular did not hesitate to answer any questions the family had. Leon's son, Lamar, said later that he had never found the right way to ask anyone (including physicians) how the bowels and bladder react when the body relaxes at death. The counselor explained the process and assured Lamar that hospice workers would help the family prepare the body. Most people find it difficult to talk about what happens to the body at death, but hospice workers are trained to enable you to do that with dignity.

Give Permission to Your Parents to Die When the Time Comes
How can you know when a person is very near death? Dying people often go through some clear and predictable stages, just like a person going through grief. And as in grief, these stages may overlap or cycle. They include the following:

- *Depression.* This can often be effectively treated with medication or counseling.
- *Anorexia.* The person has no appetite. This is the body's attempt to reduce its need for nutrition.
- *Dehydration.* Body fluids become depleted. The loss of body fluids, together with less food, helps release the natural endorphins which aid in reducing pain.
- *Drowsiness and Unarousable Sleep.* Doctors assume that the patient may still be aware of everything being said and done in the room even though the person appears to be asleep.

- *Agitation and Restlessness.* Moaning and groaning often occur during the last few minutes of life. If the person appears to be in pain, ask that he or she be given more medication.[5]

When people are dying, their world becomes very small, particularly if they are confined to bed. If alert, they tend to focus inwardly, reviewing their lives and talking about their beliefs and values. Material things cease to be important. They may even appear to be withdrawing from family to search for inward peace. Loved ones who accept the fact of dying and even give their permission for it offer great comfort to the dying.

Jeanne's mother was terminally ill with cancer and, in spite of her medications, in constant pain. She told Jeanne that the price of living had become greater than the price of dying, and she was ready to let go. However, she felt terribly guilty about "quitting" on life when it would let her family down. Once Jeanne realized that in the midst of intense suffering her mother was desperately trying to live only for the family's sake, she told her, "It's OK, Mom. I understand that you need to go." Her mother died peacefully shortly thereafter. Children often need to give their dying parents verbal permission to relinquish life when the parent feels he or she is ready to do so.

When the time comes, are you and your family willing and able to bring your parents into your home for hospice care? If so, talk with them about that option now. Death is as much a part of life as is birth and everything in between. When we accept the inevitable, we find peace—and may help our parents find it as well. As Psalm 116:15 reminds us, "Precious in the sight of the Lord is the death of his saints."

Chapter Ten

HELP! I'M OUT OF OXYGEN!

Caring for Ourselves as Caregivers

Before every airline flight, the flight attendant announces where the emergency exits are and gives information about what to do if there is an emergency. Part of her talk is always, "If the airplane should decompress for any reason, oxygen masks will fall in front of your faces. If you are traveling with children or older adults, cover your own nose and mouth first, then attend to those traveling with you." Why are adults instructed to give themselves oxygen first? Because we cannot help others if we have fainted from lack of oxygen ourselves!

Caregivers sometimes feel out of breath from handling the numerous demands on their time and emotions. If you don't give yourself "oxygen," you may burn out. In her book *Welcome to the Sandwich Generation*, Marsha Levine lists these seven signals of burnout for caregivers of elderly parents:

- Not eating properly (or changes in normal diet)
- Becoming more emotional than normal

- Feeling overwhelmed
- Starting to withdraw
- Interacting less with peers
- Having less mental focus at work
- Having a disheveled, unkempt appearance[1]

If you see one or more of these signs in you or your spouse, you may be in need of more "oxygen." In order to be sure you are getting the level of care you need, be sure that you do the following:

1. Take time on a regular basis for Bible study, prayer, or contemplation to stay spiritually replenished. "Be still, and know that I am God" (Psalm 46:10), we are instructed.

Research has shown that caregivers who used religious or spiritual beliefs to cope with caregiving demands had better relationships with the people they were caring for. In addition, those caregivers experienced less depression and anger.[2] We must not shortchange ourselves spiritually in the service of others.

Caroline and her younger sister, Cheryl, had been raised in a Christian family. Caroline, however, had developed a much more personal relationship with God. When their father died, both Caroline and Cheryl tried to help their mother, but Cheryl's attempts seemed grudging, and she became judgmental and critical of her mom. She considered caretaking a chore and pushed to have her mother placed in a care facility long before it was necessary.

Caroline, on the other hand, found that her faith gave her a different perspective. Allowing God's love to work through her, she considered caretaking an opportunity to spend time with and appreciate her mom. You, too, can plug in your faith to find strength to offer your parents loving care.

2. *Take care of yourself physically.* Get plenty of sleep, exercise regularly (even if you hate it!), eat plenty of fruits and vegetables, drink at least eight glasses of water a day, and take vitamins.

3. *Make sure your priorities are balanced.* It's a good idea to check weekly to see if you are spending your time well. Ask yourself: How are my kids doing? How many things can I eliminate that are causing me stress? How is my physical health? Am I too distracted to keep my marriage healthy? You want to make sure your marriage outlasts your parents.

4. *Find or start a support group for people dealing with elderly parents.* Check your Yellow Pages or call your local United Way agency for lists of these groups. If thinking of starting a group of your own, check with friends, church members, neighbors, doctors' offices, or even senior centers to determine if there are other families in your situation. You can begin with a simple discussion group to provide mutual understanding and support.

5. *Educate yourself about the specific challenges you and your parents face.* Information sources include physicians and attorneys. Use your parent's physician as a resource. If you are

accompanying your parent on checkups, make a list of questions to which you need answers. Be aware of community resources and plug into them. The Internet sites noted in Appendix B continuously update information about available resources for caring for the elderly. Consider taking out a subscription to *Modern Maturity* to increase your understanding of the problems of the elderly and to help you locate additional resources.

6. Keep a written schedule for tracking future events and appointments for your parents and other family members. If you don't normally keep a schedule, consider doing so. My daughter Wendy has three boys under the age of twelve, two of whom live for baseball in the summer. Wendy has a master schedule, approximately the size of Rhode Island, that tells her what she needs to be doing all the time.

If you are in charge of your own and your family's schedules—as well as that of your parents—a written schedule will help you stay organized. If you write down what you need to do and when, you'll worry less and be less likely to forget.

7. Schedule a date night with your spouse or a night out with friends on a regular basis.

8. Laugh and keep your sense of humor. If you have a person in your life who makes you laugh a lot, be sure to spend time with that person. Laughter will replenish your spirit and make you feel better.

We love this story from one of Kathy's friends, Pat. Her brother and his wife had been caring for Pat's mom, who had Alzheimer's, in their home. One night they woke to find Mom very agitated, convinced a rapist was after her. After they calmed her down, they escorted her back to her room and found every shoe she owned piled on the bed. (She loved shoes, so there were a lot of them!) The shoes, she said, were to keep the rapist away. Instead of getting irritated, sad, or frustrated, Pat's brother and sister-in-law moved the shoes off the bed, tucked Mom in, retreated to the living room, and cracked up!

9. When you need a break, ask for help from other family members. Here are some tips on how to encourage the rest of the family to share in the caregiving:

- Ask them—in person. Remind them that you need breaks.
- Give them specific tasks you need completed and let them choose one.
- Be unavailable occasionally. Give other family members plenty of notice.
- Be as organized as possible to make it easy for someone else to step in.
- Have your parents call family members and remind them they haven't been by.
- Ask for financial assistance if needed.

- Remind them that these people are their parents, too, and they will not want to regret spending too little time with them when they are gone.

10. Ask for help from friends, your own or your parents' church, or professional caregivers.

11. Identify and accept your feelings of grief and sadness. Schedule time to speak with a minister or counselor about your own mental and emotional health.

Don't Give in to Guilt

Isn't guilt a wonderful thing? Many people seem invested in making us feel guilty over our choices for our elderly parents. If we ask enough people for their opinion, we are bound to find someone willing to send us on a guilt trip for what we have or haven't done.

Martin's father deteriorated rapidly after he had a minor stroke. He had fallen a couple of times, wasn't eating well, seemed oblivious to personal hygiene, and refused to follow his doctor's recommendations. Martin and his wife, Alice, had talked with his father about moving into an assisted living situation, but he had angrily refused.

Martin and Alice had two teenagers and a younger disabled son who required constant attention. They were also career missionaries who lived in South America and were in the United States for just a few months before they returned to the mission field. They needed to find a resolution quickly.

When they asked nearby relatives if they could check in on Martin's dad every few days, no one was willing. Instead, they criticized Martin for not being willing to relocate his family back to the States in order to help his dad. Such a move would have entailed Martin giving up his lifelong work in the mission field, but his relatives implied that Martin was not being a faithful son because he was unwilling to leave that work. His relatives didn't have any problem leaving Martin with a load of guilt while at the same time abandoning him and his father.

Martin and Alice finally stopped discussing their problem with family members. They had been asking for help, which was good, but they had been asking the wrong people. The decision about what to do with his dad needed to be preceded by another decision: what was best for Martin and Alice's family. Only after answering that could they make a decision about what they needed to do for Martin's dad.

Eventually they were able to find a live-in caretaker whom they trusted. Costs for this service vary by region as well as by the level of training of the caretaker, but this option is usually much less costly than an assisted care facility. They also arranged for people from the church to set up a schedule for bringing meals by, taking his father to church and community events, and spending time with him. And Martin refused to feel guilty just because his relatives were selfishly unwilling to help.

Are You Getting the Oxygen You Need?

If you are getting the self-care you need, you will stay mentally healthy. On a practical level, this means that:

- Your life is balanced between work, family, alone time, and recreation.
- You empathize with others but recognize your limitations in responding to their needs. You recognize you can only do the best you can do.
- You laugh and find joy in life.
- You adapt to change as necessary.
- You are able to transcend sorrow and suffering.
- You have an active spiritual life.
- You are able to find meaning and purpose in life.

Many middle generation folks are reluctant to ask for help. You are taught to be self-motivated, self-sufficient, and self-reliant. But when there's not enough oxygen to go around, you may have to borrow some from others. Most of us feel complimented when people ask us to help them—and we should return the favor! When I broke my ankle, I asked a friend to take me downtown to a meeting. My friend told me later that she had been fearful of driving in downtown traffic, but she was so pleased that I'd asked for her help, she was able to overcome her fear. Everyone got extra oxygen that day.

Both Kathy and I love Isaiah 40:30-31. "Even the youths shall faint and be weary ... but they that wait upon the Lord shall renew their strength; they shall mount up with wings as eagles; they shall run, and not be weary; and they shall walk, and not faint."

Please—do whatever it takes to keep yourself well!

FINAL PERSPECTIVES

From Grace:

I'm old. I don't like being old! And there's nothing I can do about it, which I like even less.

When did it happen, this getting old?

I didn't feel old in my fifties. And when I turned sixty, I celebrated with two huge parties. Our mayor gave me a framed certificate and designated September 11, 1986, as Grace Ketterman Day. I was no longer middle-aged, but I certainly was not old.

When I turned seventy, our children planned an elegant, staggered open house party that enabled me to enjoy a host of longtime friends. I still didn't consider myself old—not until a few months later, when I learned that I had adult-onset diabetes and was developing cataracts in both eyes. I also began to sense some stiffness and even pain in many of my joints. Funny, I'd never known how many joints our bodies have until they started to hurt!

My hair began to thin in spots. I'd never realized that women as well as men can lose hair that never regrows. And although my hairdresser used a special color that removed a few years from my appearance, I knew those roots were very white.

I've never minded the crow's-feet around my eyes. They reflect the humor and good will I've worked all my life to develop. But now my eyelids droop some, and the wrinkles in the skin on my neck have wrinkles. Should I have plastic surgery? This *might* improve my aging appearance; on the other hand, I've seen victims of plastic surgery who looked as if they had Asian ancestors. Now, I love and respect my Asian friends, but I'm not Asian! Besides, even surgery could not really change the truth: I'm old. Not just *getting* old—I tried that thought for a long time! I'm *old*.

I still do a great deal of public speaking, and I'm fearful that a "senior moment" may cause me to forget my point or freeze my flow of thoughts. I write down names and events and take my vitamin E religiously to make sure I don't forget what I need to remember. The truth is, I can compensate if I happen to forget what I wanted to say, but I hate having to.

I take a tiny box full of pills every day—and I thank God for them. They provide daily health and prolong the life I love. Yet I hate to be bound by and to them!

I may not like being old, but I also realize that being old has its blessings. And these are genuine, not rationalizations. I have a warehouse full of memories. Many are starkly painful, but I survived them. The years of poverty during the Great Depression and the Midwest dust storms were terrifying. My family learned how to get along with little money but lots of love and sacrifice. The losses of my brother in a farm accident, my grandmother from a stroke, and an aunt from equine encephalitis, all in a six-month span, devastated my family and me, yet we learned to value and comfort each other. We made it through and the grief is past, leaving a certain indomitable will to survive life's next onslaught of loss and grief.

During the economic recession of the early 1980s, my brother and I discussed the fears that a 25 percent interest on loans created. I've not forgotten his words: "I know people are terrified, but I'm not. We made it through the last depression and somehow we'll do it again." He was right.

Having worked as a people helper all my life, I have had to become a thinker. I ponder the waxing and waning of American culture. Having lived through seven and a half decades, I can trace the evolution of the breakdown of families, the excessive focus on sex, and the escalation of violence in our culture.

I'm tragically unable to stop the dizzying downward spiral of values and morality in this country, but I do understand much of it. In knowledge there is some strength. I am also optimistic that God is still in charge and will swing back the pendulum from evil to good!

It's a surprising pleasure to return to my old farm home and the cemetery nearby. There rest all the relatives I have loved and lost. And there I resurrect the rich memories of all they instilled in me and know that bits of each of them live on in me.

I love looking at my children and cherishing all the lessons they so laboriously taught me. I search for evidence that I've taught them, too, hoping that I've passed on to them the treasures my family gave me. And guess what? I do find that evidence, and it blesses me!

I am grateful for a heart that cares and the training that enables me to alleviate pain. I feel a sense of elation when I meet someone who says, "Dr. Grace, I heard you speak on parenting twenty-five years ago. Your ideas worked. I appreciate what you taught me."

How delightful it is to have my four grandsons give me big bear hugs, go to lunch with me, and remind me of the time when their parents were my little kids. It's fun to tell them of the first TV I ever saw, just as I was amazed at my grandmother's story of the very first telephone in her community.

Like it or not, old age happens. We can allow it to make us helpless or grouchy, or mellow and ever more wise and loving. Within the limits of my capabilities, I intend to live to the fullest every day I'm given. I love life with all of its joys—and yes, even its sorrows.

I hope that you in the sandwich generation will find role models, hopefully in your own parents, to help you look forward to your "golden" years!

From Kathy:

I'm middle-aged. Like my mother, I'm not sure when that happened. I remember the year I was a den mother for my son's Cub Scout group. I felt entirely too young to be a den mother. Until recently, I felt I was a twenty-five-year-old trapped in a much older body. Now I think I'm a forty-eight-year-old trapped in that same body, and it's a better place to be.

Not long ago, my sister called me with some worries about one of her children. When she asked what was going on in my life, I said, "You know, as of right this minute, I'm not worrying about anything."

The greatest thing about being part of the sandwich generation is learning to appreciate those on either side of me. I appreciate and value everything my parents have taught me and everything they have stood for, and for the contributions they continue to make to my life. I have a great relationship with my son, who inherited my (and his grandfather's) sense of humor. It is fascinating to see bits and pieces of my family and his dad's family in him.

Another great thing about being this age is that I can stop struggling with the need to constantly improve myself. I no longer berate myself for all the things I'm not. I am more aware than anyone of my limitations; I am still working in small ways on some of them. But others I have just learned to accept. I've learned to accept as well that God loves me the way I am. I don't have to prove anything to anyone, which is a huge relief. I'm also pretty much done justifying or explaining myself to people. I am who I am.

My mother talks about "the downward spiral of our culture," and from her perspective, it does look downward. However, I am beginning to see small steps back from the abyss. The divorce rate in this country is beginning to drop. There are fewer teenage pregnancies. Crime rates are lowering bit by bit. I sense a renewed spiritual interest in many of my clients, particularly adolescents. And I have to give credit for these changes to my mother and others who have maintained their faith and optimism through devastating times.

Losing my parents is something I dread. But I take comfort in knowing that I've talked with them about the issues covered in this book. I take comfort in knowing that parts of them continue in me and in my son. My parents and I have done what we can to prepare, and in the meantime we're doing our best to enjoy each other. I hope that you pursue the opportunity to do the same with your parents.

Notes

TWO
When Even Down Looks Up

1. James W. Jefferson, M.D. and John R. Greist, M.D., *Depression and Older People: Recognizing Hidden Signs and Taking Steps Toward Recovery* (New York: Pfizer U.S. Pharmaceuticals, 1998).
2. Elizabeth Kubler-Ross, M.D., *On Death and Dying* (New York: Macmillan, 1969).
3. David Burns, M.D., *Feeling Good: The New Mood Therapy* (New York: Avon, 1999).

FOUR
Is Your Doctor on Speed Dial?

1. Merck Research Laboratories, *Merck Manual,* 17th ed. (Whitehouse Station, N.J.: Merck Research Laboratories, 1999), 1466–70.

FIVE
Does the Underwear Go on the Inside or the Outside?

1. Merck Research Laboratories, 73.
2. O. Madeleine Nash, "The New Science of Alzheimer's," *Time Magazine,* July 17, 2000, 51.
3. Christine Gorman, "The Three Stages of Alzheimer's," *Time Magazine,* July 17, 2000, 57.

NINE

It's My Party, I Can Die If I Want To

1. Mark Matousek, "The Last Taboo," *Modern Maturity*, September–October 2000, 49–59.
2. John Cloud, "A Kinder, Gentler Death," *Time Magazine*, September 18, 2000, 60.
3. Cloud, 60–61.
4. From Jim Towey in "Five Wishes," *Modern Maturity* September–October 2000, 97.
5. "The Body Speaks," *Modern Maturity*, September–October 2000, 53.

TEN

Help! I'm Out of Oxygen!

1. Marsha J. Levine, *Welcome to the Sandwich Generation* (P.O. Box 1694, Skokie, IL 60076, 1999).
2. Bei-Hung Chang, Anne E. Noonan, and Sharon L. Tennstedt, "The Role of Religion/Spirituality in Coping With Caregiving for Disabled Elders," *Gerontologist*, 38(4): 463–70.

APPENDIX A

Selected Bibliography

Burns, David, M.D. *Feeling Good: The New Mood Therapy.* New York: Avon, 1999.

Byock, Ira. *Dying Well: Peace and Possibilities at the End of Life.* New York: Berkley, 1997.

Chang, Bei-Hung, Anne E. Noonan, and Sharon L. Tennstedt. "The Role of Religion/Spirituality in Coping With Caregiving for Disabled Elders." *Geronotologist* 38(4): 463–70.

Cloud, John. "A Kinder, Gentler Death." *Time Magazine,* September 18, 2000.

Glasser, William. *Choice Theory: A New Psychology of Personal Freedom.* New York: Harper Collins, 1999.

Ilardo, Joseph A., and Carole R. Rothman. *I'll Take Care of You: A Practical Guide for Family.* Oakland, Calif.: New Harbinger Publications, 1999.

Jaffe, Marie. *Geriatric Nutrition and Diet Therapy.* Albany, N.Y.: Delmar Publishers, 1998.

Jefferson, James W., M.D., and John R. Greist, M.D.
Depression and Older People: Recognizing Hidden Signs and Taking Steps Toward Recovery. New York: Pfizer U.S. Pharmaceutical, 1998.

Kingsmill, Suzanne, and Benjamin Schlesinger. *The Family Squeeze: Surviving the Sandwich Generation.* Toronto: Univ. of Toronto Press, 1998.

Kubler-Ross, Elizabeth, M.D. *On Death and Dying.* New York: Macmillan, 1969.

Levine, Marsha J. *Welcome to the Sandwich Generation.* Skokie, Ill.: Marsha J. Levine, 1999.

Merck Research Laboratories. *Merck Manual,* 17th ed. Whitehouse Station, N.J.: Merck Research Laboratories, 1999.

Nash, O. Madeleine. "The New Science of Alzheimer's." *Time Magazine,* July 17, 2000.

O'Brien, Dominic. *Learn to Remember.* San Francisco: Chronicle Books, 2000.

Olshevski, Jodi L., Anne D. Katz, and Bob G. Knight. *Stress Reduction for Caregivers.* Philadelphia: Brunner/Mazel, 1999.

Sahelian, Ray, M.D. *Mind Boosters.* New York: St. Martin's Press, 2000.

Schlenker, Eleanor D. *Nutrition in Aging.* New York: McGraw-Hill, 1997.

Unell, Barbara C., and Jerry L. Wyckoff. *The Eight Seasons of Parenthood.* New York: Random House, 2000.

Weil, Andrew, M.D. *Eating Well for Optimum Health: The Essential Guide to Food, Diet and Nutrition.* New York: Knopf, 2000.

Whitaker, Julian, M.D. *The Memory Solution.* Garden City Park, New York: Avery, 1999.

Zal, H. Michael. *The Sandwich Generation: Caught Between Growing Children and Aging Parents.* New York: Insight Books/Plenum Press, 1992.

APPENDIX B

Relevant Internet Web Sites

www.uslivingwillregistry.com: Confidential service that registers your advance directives and faxes copies to hospitals when needed

www.aarp.org: American Association of Retired Persons

www.abanet.org: American Bar Association; site includes a section for senior law

www.agingwithdignity.org: Advocates for the elderly and their care givers

www.aoa.dhhs.gov/agingsites/state.html: Information about state agencies on aging

www.careguide.net: Elder care resource that offers nursing home information by state

www.caremanager.org: Geriatric Care Manager

www.grandtrvl.com: Multi-generational vacation ideas

www.hospice-america.org: Consumer's guide to hospice care

www.ianet.org: Interactive Aging Network; provides helpful resources for organizations that serve older adults

www.medicare.gov: Medicare information

www.medicare.gov/publications: Medicare publications

www.partnershipforcaring.com: 24-hour hotline with counseling, pain management tips, and advance directive samples to download

www.pbs.org/onourownterms: Dialog about end of life issues

www.seniorlaw.com: Senior Law Home Page; information about elder law, Medicare, Medicaid, estate planning, trusts, and the rights of the elderly and disabled for senior citizens, families, attorneys, social workers, and financial planners